Completing the Circle

Completing the Circle

by

Thomas Poplawski

AWSNA

Printed with support from the Waldorf Curriculum Fund

Published by:
The Association of Waldorf Schools
of North America Publications
3911 Bannister Road
Fair Oaks, CA 95628

Title: *Completing the Circle*
Author: Thomas Poplawski
Editor: David Mitchell
Proofreader: Ann Erwin
Cover: Hallie Wootan
Cover Photograph: Meg Fisher
© 2006 by AWSNA
ISBN # 1-888365-72-2

Table of Contents

The Schooling of Angels 7

Button up Your Overcoat 11

Losing Our Senses 17

Taming the Media Monster 25

The Power of Play 33

Toys Are Not Us
Escaping from the Maw of Consumerism 41

Children and Sports – Finding a Balance 49

Etheric? Asral? Ego?
An Esoteric View of the Human Being and Its
Value in the Education of the Child 57

Paradise Lost: The Nine-Year Change 71

The Four Temperaments 79

Watching Your Temper(ament) 93

A Modern Path of Meditation and Inner Development 103

The Schooling of Angels

An angel comes down to earth, conceived and received within the womb of her mother. There she grows the garments for her new home, and henceforth, she will wear the heavy robe of a physical body. After the months that this process takes, she emerges into a startling world of bright lights, cacophonous sounds and strong smells. With that first breath of terrestrial air, a visitor of timeless pure being is born into the temporal matter of earth. And with the tasting of mother's milk, so begins the education of this angel we now call *child*. For in this sweet substance of milk, the child first brings the outside world into herself. Then begins the delicate process of negotiating the needs of her new body with the rarified impulses of her angelic nature, a process supported by someone already very much of this world. As the mother adjusts to the style of the child's feeding—which already reveals a glimmer of the little one's unique personality—so begins the guiding and training of a new human being.

During the following years, this heavenly child takes on a dual citizenship of the earth. The question arises: How can we assist this child on her journey? How do we honor her heavenly origin while simultaneously ensuring that she is prepared for the travails and challenges of life in the material world? How do we cultivate strong and anchored roots in this world while protecting the delicate wings she brought along with her on this journey? Asked still another way the question is: How do we prepare a child to thrive in our fast-paced, technologically-sophisticated, and hyper-competitive world while respecting her unique gifts, her unique destiny, her calling?

A person uniquely suited to addressing these questions was the founder of Waldorf education, Rudolf Steiner, because he possessed the rare gift of being able to know clearly the reality of both worlds, temporal and spiritual, which the child inhabits.

Steiner was born in 1861 in a small, rural village in Croatia which was then part of the Austro-Hungarian Empire. His father worked for the state railway system. At that time, the train station with its telegraph office represented the leading edge of technology. The academically gifted young boy was fascinated by science and technology. His father envisioned a future in the sciences for his eldest son. When Rudolf was to begin high school, his father managed to get transferred to a posting near Vienna, allowing his son to attend a better school.

In his autobiography, Steiner describes another aspect of his early life. Steiner relates that as a child he had a natural gift of clairvoyance or spiritual sight. He experienced meeting recently deceased relatives, as well as other spiritual phenomena, but at the time he learned to say little about this. These experiences moved him very deeply and were to create a foundation for some of his later life's work.

After finishing high school, Steiner attended the scientific university in Vienna, the *Technische Hochschule,* the M.I.T. of Central Europe at that time. His studies prepared him to become a university-level professor of science, though his life path took another direction. His first major position was in Weimar where he had been invited to edit the scientific works of the famous German writer and poet, Johann Wolfgang von Goethe. Steiner appreciated Goethe's vision of the spiritual element that lies within nature and found it to be a life-long inspiration.

During his seven years in Weimar, Steiner also completed a doctoral dissertation in philosophy. He had continued to wrestle with the polarity of a scientific and a spiritual view of reality, and this struggle culminated in his writing what he later considered to be his most important book, *The Philosophy of Spiritual Activity*. In this work he explored how intellectual thinking is a first step toward an enhanced thinking which is able to penetrate the boundary into spiritual realms. A human being can experience true freedom only in the clarity of thinking which is inspired not by the instinctual realm of our earthly desires and emotions but by intuitions from the spirit. Steiner used these insights as a basis for all of his later practical work in the arts, the sciences and the social-economic realm. The field for which he is most famous today, however, is in the field of education. Here Steiner focused on the questions we have posed above.

These questions are an obvious reframing of the Nature versus Nurture debate. The reframing occurs in the expansion of the meaning of Nature to include not only the hereditary aspects of the child's being but also its spiritual heritage. In the series of articles presented in this book, we begin with the concept of "protection." The developing child from birth all the way to adulthood needs the help of parents and teachers to form a protective circle about the delicate wings of his inner being. This protection has many aspects. The child obviously needs to be sheltered from the physical elements so that physically he can flourish. However, some of the qualities of modern life—the rapid pace, the materialistic worldview and the impact of new technologies—have introduced new dangers to challenge a child's neurological and emotional well-being.

The child finds his footing in the world through the magical activity of play. However, modern life has erected obstacles even to this archetypal children's activity. We will look at the nature of play and how the Waldorf schools seek to promote that which helps the child to grow and, if needed, to heal. We will also look at how the toys we surround children with and the sports activity we introduce them to can interfere with the healthy instinct for play in the child.

Alas, raising and educating children is not all just about angels. We also need to deal with the demons. In the second section of the book we will look at the challenges within the three different stages of childhood. From the perspective of the non-physical "bodies" of the child, we will look at what goes on in these stages of development and then continue by focusing on the transition that occurs in a child's life between ages nine and ten. We will also look at the topic most looked for in a book about raising children: discipline.

Next, we will explore an aspect of both children and adults that is connected to both our spiritual and hereditary nature, that of the temperaments. Looking not only at the personality type of our children but that of ourselves is an exercise that truly brings us down to earth.

We strive to surround our children with a circle of warmth, protection, and wholesome influences. This allows them the freedom to unfold their unique gifts, to find their special path. In building this circle we are required to make wise choices and then find the strength and perseverance to carry them out despite those forces in the world which are not child-affirming. We find some of this wisdom and strength through the support of like-minded parents and teachers. However, sometimes our circle also needs to include the wider community of angels. Connecting with the wellspring of human creativity and inspiration in the realm of the spirit is a core principle of all of Rudolf Steiner's work. In our concluding chapter we look at how developing this connection is possible through the fostering of a spiritual practice of meditation. All of the past contributions as well as the future development of Waldorf education depend on remaining open to this source of life-enhancing energy. As parents, we might also find completion by making this connection a part of our lives as well.

Button up Your Overcoat

There is a "folk wisdom" which remains alive in the Waldorf community but that is increasingly neglected in the larger society. It concerns how children, on many levels need to be protected. Waldorf parents are encouraged to shield their children from the mass media and technology, from adolescent and adult fashions in clothes and from junk and convenience foods—not too many sweets in the lunchbox, please.

There is another caution which is often neglected because to many it seems so minor. For near the top of the list of "Waldorf wisdom" is taking special care to keep infants and children physically warm.

The fetus at birth leaves the totally protected, warm, dark environment of the womb. It is thrust into a relatively cold world full of dazzling lights, harsh sounds, and often chaotic stimuli. The newborn, expelled from paradise, needs a period of transition to get used to its new environment. Thus a mother will instinctively hold the infant close, enveloping it physically in her arms. In doing so, she is enveloping it on a more subtle level, within her aura, within the protective covering of her life energies and soul warmth. If she needs to set the baby down, she needs to wrap it warmly, cover its head snugly with a knitted cap, and lay the infant in a warm, secure place. Keeping an infant warm is especially important because the ability to regulate body temperature has not yet been established. The newborn has a very large head in comparison to the rest of the body. Since most body heat is lost through the head, it is crucial that the infant's head be covered with a cap of cotton, wool or silk. The cap also serves to cover the tender fontanel, that place at the top of the skull where the bones have not yet come together. It protects too from the direct rays of the sun, which for the infant can also be too extreme.

This wrapping and covering of the baby—which has its parallel with the older child—has significance beyond mere physical warmth. In many religions there is the tradition of covering the head for church or temple. At play here is the intuition that to protect and keep the head warm is to keep the soul "warm," to keep it from hardening and thereby unreceptive to spirit. In the child, this protection of the "warmth organism" supports the development of emotional flexibility and fluidity. On a warm, sunny day, a mother may feel that she does not need a head covering, but it is still important to protect the much more sensitive baby.

The newborn must also be guarded from a too rapid exposure to the bright lights, activity, and commotion of the everyday world. Traditionally, a mother observed a "lying-in" period, during which she and the infant remained in a curtained room where light was dim and filtered. This gave the infant's eyes—and emotional being—time to develop and to be able to focus. (Placing a rose-colored silk cloth over the crib as a canopy can give a similar protection.) This period of relative dark and quiet usually lasted a number of weeks—forty days in some cultures. During this period the mother rested and bonded with the child with limited distraction. Only the closest of family and friends came to visit, and there was no question of taking the baby out during this somewhat sacred time.

Alas, what a far cry from the situation today! Now one sees a two- or three-day-old child, dazed and vulnerable, being paraded around one's office or wheeled around beneath the glare of fluorescent lights in a noisy shopping mall. We have largely forgotten and lost the old practice of sheltering the newborn.

Fortunately many mothers today retain an intuitive sense that the newborn must be protected from cold, from the harshness of the summer sun, and from sensory over-stimulation. However, few realize just how long this "gesture of the womb" continues to be an important need for the child, especially as regards the aspect of warmth.

Warmth and the Growing Child

As the child matures, the body has a finite amount of energy to use for growth, both for the growth of the body as a whole and for the development of the brain and inner organs. Keeping the body warm allows the greatest amount of these energies to be devoted to this task. When the child is not sufficiently warm, these other areas can be shortchanged because the growth forces are used up just in trying to keep warm. Paying special attention to keeping Johnny's hat on, scarf wrapped, and coat buttoned are therefore important for more than just fending off colds. They allow the child to devote all available energies to his healthy growth and development. Whether hats are in or out of fashion at the moment, the growing child should wear one and should otherwise be kept warm.

Some pediatricians advise that you should have your child dress with as many layers as you yourself need. The problem with this is that adults have much greater control of body temperature and often a greater store of bodily fat. A child tends to be more like an elderly person, who is in "second childhood" and who does not retain body heat. The difference, though, is that a child can be turning blue with the cold and have chattering teeth and not even realize that he or she is cold.

Temperament is also a factor which should be mentioned. The choleric parent can often be less sensitive to temperature while the melancholic child has an especial need for extra layers, both to warm his often spare frame as well as serving to give these often anxious and overly-sensitive children an extra buffer from the world—a security blanket. All children through the age of thirteen or fourteen can benefit, especially in their more vulnerable moments, from an extra layer of clothing. It is no coincidence that we speak of the loving care that we give to others as warmth.

Three above and Two below

One frosty March New England morning when I took my sons to school, one of their classmates took off his winter coat to reveal that all he wore underneath was a T-shirt! As the door opened again admitting the next chilling blast of wind, I inwardly shivered, though this little fellow did not seem to notice at all. Then a seven-year-old girl came in with the tiniest of thin skirts and bare legs and a thin unbuttoned cardigan. Brrr!

One Waldorf school doctor recommends that as long as it is below 60 degrees, all children should wear—in addition to their coats—at least three layers above and two below. All layers, however, are not created equal. The Europeans have long favored wearing wool as one of those layers, especially for underwear, finding it superior to all other fabrics for promoting warmth. Thus optimally a child might wear cotton underwear, followed by a wool undergarment (or tights) and then warm pants or a skirt and a shirt. On very cold days, especially for the slim or delicate child, a woolen vest or sweater might be worn as well. Socks and caps should be of wool.

"What is so special about wool?" you may ask. It is not usually available at local stores, may require special care in washing and drying, and so on. Wool is an amazing fabric, though. It can absorb up to thirty percent of its own weight in moisture without feeling damp. Also, it wicks moisture away from the skin and insulates when wet. Thus a child with wet wool socks will still have warm feet. Duofold, which is generally available and which has an inner cotton layer and an outer woolen one, is an excellent option.

Synthetic fabrics like polypropylene and polyester fleece have some of wool's characteristics, but they impact the environment negatively in their manufacture and disposal. Also, as artificial fabrics (fleece is made from recycled plastic soda bottles), they lack wool's natural aesthetic appeal. They just "feel" peculiar and "unnatural." On the more subtle level they may be detrimental to the child's developing senses (see the chapter "Losing Our Senses"). In the totally nonscientific but perhaps deeply intuitive view of one art therapist, "Fleece is entirely dead, carrying deadening vibrations and not what you want to wrap your child in if you can help it!" And most of us can help it.

The archetypal image of the robed Madonna holding, enveloping, and protecting her young child is an image we all need to hold and nurture as we go about our own not-so-archetypal lives. Keeping our children well-covered and warm from head to foot is sometimes a struggle but a very important part of this picture. In the words of a popular tune of the 1940s:

Button up your overcoat,
It's beginning to freeze;
Take good care of yourself,
You belong to me...

Losing Our Senses

When the actor Tony Danza was asked about his view of parenting, he replied:

Hold back the tide. Keep your kids innocent as long as possible. It's like a dike and you've got your fingers and toes in the holes, holding back an unending flood of inappropriate information.

Danza's concern for his two young daughters echoes the sentiments of many parents today. We need to protect our children physically in an increasingly violent world. But we need to protect them emotionally and psychologically also—from the danger of growing up too soon. We need to shield them from developmentally inappropriate materials, from adult language, sexuality, fashion, and the media. Our children are in danger of prematurely losing their childhood. But, there is another, perhaps greater danger. Our children are at risk of losing their very senses of perception.

The Rational Psychology Association (*Gesellschaft für Rationelle Psychologie* or *GRP*) in Munich, Germany, has been conducting research for several decades on the processing of stimuli in the brain and the emotions. Some four thousand subjects are involved in the study. About twenty years ago researchers began to note a striking phenomenon: the receptivity of the senses of smell and taste was deteriorating significantly. According to psychologist Henner Ertel:

The brain had set a new sensation threshold, so to speak, and refused to recognize sensations below this new limit, sensations that would have been unconditionally accepted before.

This seeming trend was not yet considered remarkable until the 1980s, when deterioration in the other senses began to be evident. Ertel reported with concern:

Suddenly all of the senses were impaired. The brain refused to take any action on a significant proportion of the stimuli. It was getting more and more difficult to stimulate the corresponding centers in the cerebral cortex.

Still the research team at GRP was not alarmed. Apparently the brain was in a process of transformation. In order to react, it now needed a barrage of stimuli which, prior to 1949, would have put an individual into shock. The brain was no doubt trying to adapt to the pace, stress, and intensity of the technological age.

This trend, however, has continued to accelerate. What finally alarmed the GRP team was the realization that the brain's sensitivity to stimuli is decreasing now at a rate of one percent a year. Subtle and delicate sensations are simply filtered out. Instead only the "brutal thrills," as the especially strong stimuli are termed, elicit any response.

One series of studies shows that optical information is being processed by this "new brain" without being evaluated. When a group of adults were shown the so-called "Flesher videos," in which people are dismembered or mutilated, their experience was one of disgust and revulsion. Most of the subjects walked out on the film. Younger people, however, shown the same video, watched without emotion and were concerned only whether the plot was exciting or not.

Other GRP studies indicate that the ability to distinguish sounds is also declining. Sixteen years ago the average German could distinguish 300,000 sounds, while today that number is only 180,000. For many children the level is only 100,000. This is enough for rap or pop music, but not for classical music, which includes many more subtle sounds. This decline in auditory sensitivity may be a major reason for the declining interest in classical music.

The sense of smell is also deteriorating and may account for changing olfactory preferences. In rural Germany, marriage proposals were often made beneath fragrant blossoming chestnut trees. Today most young people consider the fragrance repulsive.

Accompanying this decrease in sensitivity to sensory stimuli is a lessening of the pleasure derived from daily, mundane experiences. In 1971, GRP researchers began to study the enjoyment that people experienced with certain foods. They prepared a package of basic foodstuffs—bread, fish, grapefruit, coffee, and so on—and asked subjects to rate the enjoyment value of each item. Repeated at five-year intervals, this ongoing study has shown that the enjoyment ratings have moved steadily downward. Researchers note that with women the drop was not as great as with men and that those under the age of forty showed more of a decrease than those over forty. The only products that now give more pleasure than before are beer and mineral waters. The general trend, though, is that the threshold of sensation and pleasure has risen. Nothing seems to taste as good as it used to.

The researchers at GRP now feel that over the past twenty-five years the brain of the average individual has undergone significant changes in its organization. The decrease in sensitivity to sensory stimuli implies that stimuli are being processed in a different way than before. Researchers hypothesize that there are fewer cross-linkages or networks in the brain; therefore primarily optical stimuli go directly to the optical center without activating other sensory or emotional centers. Thus human beings can take in very powerful stimuli that are discordant, senseless, or contradictory without being bothered. The trend researcher Gert Gerken has labeled this phenomenon "the new indifference." Drug rehabilitation researcher, Felicitas Vogt, emphasizing the higher threshold needed to gain satisfaction, has coined the term "turbo-brain." The researchers at GRP use the more conservative term "the new brain."

One may of course respond to this phenomenon with the query: So what? The brain now has reset the level at which it reacts. This probably has happened in history at other times when great changes were taking place. Is not this just the brain's way of adapting to the realities of a new world, to our modern way of life? Our world today is full of powerful and exciting stimuli, and to deal with these we have lost sensitivity to impressions at the subtle end of the spectrum. Is this necessarily bad?

Obviously, we have changed. The speed and intensity of our time have dulled the sensitivity of every person. Children and young people have been particularly affected. Loud music, violent movies, fast computer games, shrill colors, powerful drugs are reducing our sensitivity to stimuli, so that louder music, faster and more engrossing computer games, shriller colors, more powerful drugs—legal and illegal—are necessary to grab and hold our attention, to interest, and to stimulate us. Without this hyperstimulation we are in danger of not feeling anything at all.

The world we live in is a complex and subtle one. It cannot be grasped fully by words, numbers, or reason. We can begin to truly comprehend it only through capacities of the soul that involve calm, sensitivity, and refinement. Traditionally these capacities were schooled through observation of and contact with the subtle beauties of the natural world and through the practice of the arts. Once the most treasured of human capacities, these are now being subverted and destroyed. The new brain begins to lose connection with this entire realm. Incapable of responding to subtle stimuli, it must be thrilled. Gentleness, calm, sensitivity—these are attributes that do not apply to the new brain.

Boredom and depression increase. Because the "little things in life" no longer delight, and because delicate and soft perceptions and feelings are less possible (leaving only sentimentality), the perceived world becomes ever more empty, ever less able to stimulate interest. The world must always be more radically and more artificially enhanced in order to provide enjoyment. Ertel estimates that the new brain will completely establish itself in the West by the first half of the next century. This new brain has dangerous implications for the near and distant future.

What can we do to stop and perhaps reverse this disturbing trend? What can we do to protect and regain our own and our child's sensitivity to the world?

Today many techniques to develop "mindfulness," as well as many meditation practices based in the various religious traditions, are available. These can be a great help to adults in "keeping their senses." While the new brain will make it even more difficult to sit and practice such exercises, the variety of techniques, teachers, and aids (tapes, drumming, and so on) makes it possible for virtually everyone to find something that is appropriate and helpful.

The solution for our children needs to take another form, as true meditation is not possible until adulthood. Here are some things you can do for your children—and for yourself.

1. Unplug. Keep your child's life free of television, videos, computer games, and movies until the age of ten, and then be very careful about what and how much they experience.

For most families this is an exceedingly radical recommendation, because we are addicted to the media. The oft-heard justification that there are many educational programs on television and that computers can foster learning is something like the alcoholic citing the nutritional aspects of beer. Content is only a small part of the problem with electronic media. For young adults, exploration of the possibilities of media and computers may be desirable, but in the formative years when the brain is developing it is anathema. Recent research clearly shows that a child exposed to such media fails to develop neurologically in a normal and healthy way. There are many good books on this issue, for example, Jerry Mander's *Four Arguments for the Elimination of Television* and Jane Healy's *Endangered Minds: Why Our Children Can't Think and What We Can Do About It.*

2. Slow down your lifestyle and give family life the time it needs and deserves.

The concept of "quality time" has been largely discredited. It is now increasingly clear that in family life "quantity time" is crucial. We need to spend more time with our children in a regular, consistent, unhurried way. We need to sit down to dinner as a family every day (and to linger at the table), spend time in the evenings relaxing and doing things together, go out on weekend family outings, and so on. Jon Kabat-Zinn's book *Mindful Parenting* includes helpful ideas in this direction.

3. Give your child many and regular experiences of nature.

Find a place for nature in your family life. This means frequent and regular activities in the outdoors for you and your child. Take your infant out in the baby carriage for walks; play outdoors with your toddler, rain or shine; and go hiking, canoeing, and camping with your older child. Bring nature into the home with a seasonal festival table like the one found in the Waldorf classroom, on which are placed things from nature that reflect the special quality of the season. Use bouquets of flowers, twigs, and grasses to decorate your home. Grow an indoor and/or an outdoor garden. Get a pet.

4. Bring the arts into your home, and do so without the aid of electronics.

Every Waldorf first-grader learns to play the recorder, but parents—even those without musical experience—can also learn to play this lovely instrument. The informal family concerts that can then take place will provide memories cherished for life. Sing every day, ideally without radio or taped accompaniment. Paint, draw, and do beeswax or clay modeling with your little ones—and with the older ones too. Take art, dance, or even eurythmy classes yourself. Hang artwork on your walls; take the family to classical and other acoustic concerts, dance performances, and museums.

Those who have read any of the best-selling books on the life of the soul—books by Thomas Moore, Robert Sardello, and others—may find some of these suggestions familiar. To regain the sanity, equanimity, and sense of wholeness in life—which has been termed "soul"—involves a commitment to creating and protecting a sacred space in our lives. We need to work at "coming to our senses" while we still have them.

For a more in-depth report (in English) on the work of the GRP, see the article "Research into Changes in Brain Formation" by Michael Kneissle in the Waldorf Education Research Institute's *Research Bulletin*, June 1997.

Taming the Media Monster

There is a warm and cheery feeling in the room for this, the first meeting of the year for the new kindergarten parents. Sharing stories about the little angels brings laughter, and when the teacher reflects what a great step it is to send the little ones off to school for the first time, there is a bittersweet tear here and there. After a stern mini-lecture about hair lice and another laugh over what parents tend to forget to pack in the mornings, Ms. Jeffers takes a deep breath and continues: "And now I'd like to talk about another policy here at the Waldorf school that all of you heard about during your entrance interview but which is controversial for some—the school policy about television and media."

Suddenly the room is quiet and tense. It is as if an arctic wind has suddenly cut through the balmy ambiance that had moments ago filled the space. A number of parents cross their legs or arms, and others begin to squirm in their seats. Ms. Jeffers also becomes uncomfortable. The sudden change in the room is apparent to her as well—though not unexpected. Nevertheless, she forges ahead with conviction, relating her own experience of the difference between children exposed to the media and those who are not. She also cites research findings critical of television viewing and computer use by children and hands out reprints of articles and studies by respected authorities. She concludes by strongly recommending that parents protect their children from exposure to the media—in other words, no television, videos, video games, and computer activities of any kind.

But the mood of the evening is ruined, just as it is every year when this topic is brought up. Some parents leave feeling that the school's policy is extreme. One parent recently had chosen not to enroll his child, saying, "No television and no white sugar—this isn't the place for us."

Others feel that somehow their expertise and their commitment as parents are being called into question because they do not agree with the Waldorf "party line." Why, the teacher even hinted that if a child talks about *Sesame Street* or sings tunes from a Disney movie the parents would be called in for a conference. Goodness, is this some kind of Inquisition?

Other parents who nodded their heads in approval at the teacher's presentation also feel perturbed. They are indignant that some parents are threatening what is perhaps their own main aim in coming to a Waldorf school—to shelter their children from the culture (if that is indeed the right word!) of television. They seek for their children an environment characterized by spontaneous free play, wholesome games, stories, and singing, one free of unsavory media content, "trash talk," violent and distasteful imagery, and the adolescent "jive" and coolness of most so-called children's entertainment. They hope that the school community agrees on standards protecting the magical years from three to twelve.

The teacher goes home frustrated by the unsupportive response she has had from a number of families on this issue. She has seen how damaging media can be for the delicate unfolding of the young children. Yet these otherwise caring parents close a door when the topic of media comes up. She wishes there were a way to help them understand.

The Media Society

For parents who have never had their family's media use called into question, the idea of a media ban at home can seem extreme. This is especially true if they are already used to using television and DVDs to keep the children occupied when they want a moment of peace. A parent who makes a living from computers or media entertainment is likely to react even more. "What do you mean it's not good for my child?"

Almost all parents today have grown up with television. Of course, the content of television programming has changed, the amount children watch has increased, and the advent of DVDs, tape players, and computers has thickened the brew. Studies show that parents born after 1965 tend to allow their children more exposure to media than parents born earlier, presumably because they associate watching television with a warm, cozy family life. The television and increasingly the computer are felt to be, like the family dog, necessary parts of a household. Of course, everyone believes in moderation, so limiting media to a couple of hours a night seems a reasonable request. But eliminate it entirely? Whoa!

Rudolf Steiner never experienced television, but he did know about the silent movies popular in the early part of the twentieth century. Steiner recognized the medium's potential as a new art form and realized that technologically-based entertainment would develop and spread. But he was aware of the negative effects and had serious reservations about such entertainment. In a conversation with a stage designer of the time, Steiner cautioned that film corrupts people's relation to time and space and spoils their ability to have a real imagination. For these reasons, he was concerned even about adults who watch too many films.

For decades Waldorf educators have opposed all media use by children, especially young children, but communicating this to parents is more daunting than ever. The situation is analogous perhaps to that surrounding tobacco use in the 1960s. The society as a whole accepted cigarette smoking as benign, and the few people who warned about possible negative effects were dismissed as alarmists and health nuts. There were even scientific studies (paid for by the tobacco industry) which espoused some of the advantages of cigarette smoking!

Fortunately, medical and psychological researchers have come to share the concerns of Waldorf teachers. A steady stream of research has indicated the ill effects of media exposure on the child and the adult. The negative consequences include obesity, impairment of neurological development, increase in aggression, desensitization to violence, male/female stereotyping, a warping of the child's sense of reality, and susceptibility to commercialism and materialism—all from a few hours a day of "screen time."

As evidence has mounted, even the conservative American Academy of Pediatrics has asked its members to inquire how much media the children they treat are watching. Also, the Academy issued a policy statement urging that children under two years old not be allowed to watch any television at all and recommending that no child of any age have a television in his or her own bedroom or watch more than two hours a day. Some pediatricians feel that the position should be even stronger and expect that, with more research, the age at which it is thought safe for a child to watch television, videos, and so on will rise. One can see a battle brewing that may eclipse the current struggle involving the tobacco industry. While tobacco use causes many people to die prematurely, the effects of media exposure are more subtle. They include the failure of children to realize their full potential as productive and happy human beings.

The research that has most influenced pediatricians shows that babies and toddlers need almost constant direct interactions with parents and other primary caregivers. These are necessary for healthy brain growth and the development of appropriate social, emotional, and cognitive skills. As the child gets older, direct, hands-on interactions with other human beings, the environment, and with nature are critical. And it is just these interactions, necessary throughout infancy and early childhood, that do not occur when children are involved in the unnatural activity of sitting still and watching electronic signals.

For Waldorf teachers, however, concern about media use is based less on the scientific studies and more on their own experience of seeing the difference between children exposed to media and those not exposed. Celia Riahi, a Waldorf preschool teacher with many years' experience, says she can recognize the "media children" in her class through the chaotic and mechanical movements and sounds that they make, in imitation of what they have seen on television. The play of these children is impaired. They tend to get stuck in a story line or get obsessed with one particular character—usually a television character. To the preschool specialist such behavior does not portend well for later development.

Many Waldorf teachers feel that allowing a child to be exposed to the media undermines what they are trying to accomplish in the classroom. Waldorf education relies largely on the ability of the children to listen to, observe, and absorb what the teacher is saying and doing and also to respond sensitively to artistic stimuli. Media viewing shortens attention span and dulls sensory sensitivity. Here not only the activity of viewing but also of listening to electronically reproduced voice and music is problematic. Thus parents' inability to eliminate media exposure is a major problem.

Saying Farewell to an Old Friend

The Swiss physician Elisabeth Kübler-Ross is well-known for her research with terminally ill patients. She found that patients and their families go through a series of steps in dealing with the crisis of impending death. Each stage must be worked through and transcended if patient and family are to come to some peace before the end. If they become stuck somewhere in the process, there will be no resolution even though death will occur. These stages pertain not only to the loss that occurs in death but to every traumatic life change.

Families seeking to swallow the seemingly bitter pill of unplugging from media stimulation can expect a similar journey through the stages of denial, bargaining, anger, and depression. At each stage certain comments are typical.

Denial
"Television isn't a problem in our home. Our children never watch . . . well, maybe once in a while. Just a little bit during the week and then maybe on weekends a bit more."

"All the public schools are getting computers, so it must be the best thing for keeping our children ahead of the game. I love the Waldorf school, but sometimes these teachers are just too old-fashioned."

Bargaining
"How about if I limit it to one video on the weekends and give them a little more freedom during vacation times?"

Anger
"Let those teachers come here some rainy day and figure out what to do with my two boys."

"Do they expect me to stop watching television—which is the only way I have to unwind—just so the children don't watch any?"

Depression

"I just feel so miserable. How do I let those Waldorf teachers make me feel stupid and inferior and that I have already ruined my children by what I have let them watch?"

"I can't take away the kids' TV and computer. They would just hate me and think I am a horrible mom. Besides, I could never cook dinner if they didn't have a DVD or something to keep them occupied."

An objective look at the growing evidence of the harmful effects of media on the growing child should cause a caring parent to think again about media use. In fact, probably almost all Waldorf parents do try to cut back on media in the home. But they get stuck in one of these stages or crumble in the face of pressure from children, relatives, and friends. Holding out against a societal obsession is difficult. Also, it involves time and energy to find interesting things for a child to do and for a parent to do with a child. The parent's own personal space and time will be compromised.

Parents may succeed in protecting a child from the media. There is then the question as to how long this should continue. Among Waldorf teachers, responses to this question reflect a continuum from a purist position—that to some is impractical and unenforceable—through levels of compromise in bowing to what is felt to be the unstoppable force of popular culture. Almost all teachers feel that there should be no media at all before age seven. Some put this at age nine. Many then are willing to countenance judicious use of television between ages nine and twelve, with parents selecting the programs and, ideally, watching along with their children. One parent I know likes to have a Saturday family movie night watching old classics with his children ages 10 to 16 (it is always a problem what to do when you have older children who are mature enough for things their younger siblings are not.) Many teachers feel that after the onset of adolescence, at around age thirteen, the young person should have freedom in this area but also the benefit of parental guidance. Individual differences should be taken into account. For a very sensitive child of nine or ten, or older, even relatively benign classic family films like *The Wizard of Oz* or *The Sound of Music* may be frightening.

Waldorf parents who do struggle with their school's policy about the media and do work out a reasonable compromise should not be overcome by guilt or by fear of some impending disaster. There are many wholesome influences working in the life of the Waldorf child.

Still, something quite subtle may be compromised in the development of the child. Roberto Trostli is a Waldorf teacher and Waldorf teacher trainer who has taken several classes through the upper elementary grades. He comments that among graduating eighth graders, he can tell which ones still have little or no exposure to media. They are the students with the most capacity for imagination. They are the self-starters and the children in the class with the most initiative. Such an observation may be the most compelling reason for parents to take a hard look at the media question.

The Power of Play

"All they do in Waldorf kindergartens is play. The children don't learn anything."

This common if uninformed view of Waldorf kindergartens points to an important characteristic of Waldorf early childhood education: the emphasis on play. While most educational approaches today emphasize so-called "skill-building" and "school readiness" in the early years, Waldorf education considers free, imaginative play as the most important activity of the young child. Behind this is a particular view of the nature and needs of the young child, a view that is steadily gaining support from psychologists and researchers.

Free play is play in which the child—alone or with other children—uses objects in her immediate environment, creates imaginary scenes, and acts out imaginary scenarios. For example, a line of kindergarten chairs may become a bus on which the children are going for a trip to the country, or a brick may become a bulldozer that is used to create a row of "houses" in a sandbox. Free play is play without adult coaxing or direction.

For some time, psychologists and child educators have understood that through play, the toddler learns a broad range of cognitive, social, physical, and linguistic skills. This learning through play continues for three- to seven-year-olds, but in many cases the time for free play is being steadily reduced by children's increasingly busy days. It is more and more common that a child is relentlessly scheduled—from school to child care to gymnastics or ballet or Suzuki violin classes (to name but a few of the currently popular options for pre-schoolers). And what free time there is tends to be occupied by television, computer games, DVDs or recorded music. According to a study from the University of Michigan, since 1981 the portion of their time that children spend in free play has decreased from forty to less than twenty-five percent.

In school and even at home, there has been the unending effort made to give the child every possible advantage by pushing early academic learning and the early development of specific skills, this in spite of the fact that educational research has found no evidence that such early "enrichment" programming provides any long-term advantage for most children. Only disabled children and those from deprived circumstance, like those served in the Head Start program, clearly benefit from them.

It is interesting that Maria Montessori (1870-1952), founder of the Montessori educational movement, began her work in Italy with just these two groups, first with mentally retarded children, and then with children from the slums of Rome. She found children in these two groups understimulated by their environments and living too much in the realm of fantasy. In her desire to teach these children to "live on the earth," she developed a specific skills-based approach. This features a carefully prepared learning environment in which children play with or manipulate selected educational props such as alphabet boards and strings of counting beads. Montessori's distrust of free play was then carried over into the educational method which she generalized for normal children. This bias against free play has continued to this day in one segment of the Montessori movement. In classrooms belonging to the American Montessori Internationale one finds no toys and little provision for creative play. In schools belonging to the rival American Montessori Society schools, however, a break from the founder's direction has been made in this regard, and there is openness to the need for free play for the children.

A recent *Psychology Today* article blames the Puritan view that childhood should be short and dedicated to getting children to work as early as possible as one source of the prejudice against free play. The article also cites Freud's condemnation of play as an unacceptable activity in a world that should be dedicated to either work or love.

In recent decades, however, researchers have been looking carefully at the role of imaginative play in the preschool years. They are finding more and more evidence to support Rudolf Steiner's insight that play is indeed the most appropriate tool for pre-school learning.

What Children Learn through Play

A pair of psychologists, Jerome and Dorothy Singer, has been studying "fantasy play" for over twenty years. In addition to carrying out their own research, they have reviewed the entire literature on play and conclude that verbal fluency, creative or divergent thinking, and the ability to think in general are directly related to the capacity for imaginative play.

Another researcher, Sandra Russ at Case Western Reserve University found still other beneficial aspects to play. She observed that through play the child is able to take its passive experiences and work them over and over until they can be assimilated or digested. This is a function of play which is utilized by the child psychotherapist in play therapy or the Jungian sand tray work, in which the child is helped to process traumatic experiences through play. Russ concluded, however, that imaginative play is the tool that every child uses to learn to cope with stress in life and that to interfere with the child's learning how to play in a healthy manner imperils the later development of emotional regulation and coping skills.

Waldorf preschool teacher, Elizabeth Moreland of the Hartsbrook School in Massachusetts, echoes the findings of these experts. She explains that the ability to play deeply and with undivided attention is in itself a skill that a child must develop if later in life she is to learn to focus and concentrate deeply. In free play the child develops a vivid picture consciousness and then takes these pictures into doing, into action, which develops the will. The content of play comes from the environment and the gestures, physical activity and work of the adults and older children the child observes. What the child experiences and sees she then incorporates into her play. The child also attempts in play to imitate the feelings that she senses in the joy, anger, and other emotional expressions of parents and other adults. This is an important first step toward understanding and managing emotional life. Thus, it is vital that the child have sufficient time, place, and safety for play in her life.

The Child Who Could not Play

Because free play is so crucial to the healthy development of the child, it is disturbing how this archetypal aspect of childhood is being disrupted or neglected. Overscheduling of children and the attendant driving to and fro have deprived children of the time to play. There are, however, other pressures as well.

The Waldorf preschool teacher tends to become rather a connoisseur of children's play. The teacher is able to evaluate the general well-being of a child new to the class through observing his ability to play independently. Over the years, teachers have noted an increase in the number who really have difficulty playing on their own for any amount of time. In some instances, they have even encountered four- and five-year-olds who cannot play on their own. Imagine that—a child who cannot play!

The findings of the physician Stuart Brown are especially sobering in this regard. Brown was asked to investigate the background of a young man who some years ago shot and killed nineteen people from a tower at The University of Texas in Austin. He found that the man had a history of not playing in his childhood and adolescence. When Brown went on to examine the lives of other killers, he found a similar deprivation in their early years. On the other hand, when he made a study of individuals who had been awarded the famous MacArthur Foundation "genius" awards, Brown found, almost without exception, a rich background of play from childhood to adulthood. He went on to help found The Institute for Play in Carmel, California, because of his conviction that play is essential for the development of healthy individuals.

Identifying Hindrances to Play

The Waldorf teacher works therapeutically to support, encourage, and protect the delicate unfolding of play in young children, so that the myriad developmental skills arising from play and playfulness become available to them. The teachers also work with the parents to help them to understand those influences which interfere with play. The main culprits include:

1. Electronic media

These prevent young children from developing their own inner pictures. The child's later creativity depends on the early development of this skill. Instead they fill the child with artificial, not infrequently warped, images of fantasy. In one study, children's play with "super-heros" was observed and seen to be much less original and revolving perpetually around violence. Also, electronic images—so different from what the child sees and experiences in her immediate, concrete environment—are difficult for the child to assimilate and work into her understanding of everyday life. Rather than giving the child a head start, preschool computer training and "educational TV" are preventing the child from exercising the most important brain- and soul-building capacities of this stage of life. Fortunately, often just removing electronic media from a child's life is sufficient to restore healthy play.

Electronic toys are also problematic for the young child. They too can overwhelm. Also because they are quite fixed rather than open-ended, they limit the child's use of his imagination. For a child at play, a stick can become almost anything, but an electronic robot is is always just an electronic robot.

2. The adultification of the child

This is especially a danger in one-child families in which the parents are college educated. A child is by nature nonlogical and feeling-oriented, and in a household with a dominant intellectual ethos, the child's need simply to be a child may not be acknowledged let alone met. When there are more children in the household, the parents are more likely to surrender the adult orientation in the home and try to enter the very different consciousness of the children and meet their real needs. This of course is not always the case.

In an adult-oriented environment, the child is treated as another adult. She is asked too many questions, particularly about what she wants. This gives the child too much responsibility too early for making decisions, decisions for which she lacks the reason or moral sense to make. Also, the small child, in fact a dreamy little being, is given too many intellectual or scientific explanations about how things work. This burdens the child with facts and concepts that are not a part of her world yet and which she cannot digest. For example, it is much more appropriate to explain the phases of the moon to a small child by a fairy tale depicting the swallowing of the moon by a great whale than to give her a scientific explanation of how it really occurs. The fairy tale enlivens and encourages the picture-making facility. (See psychologist David Elkind's book, *The Hurried Child*, for discussion of other aspects of the issue of adultification.)

3. Emotional trauma

In most traditional cultures, the custom is that parents not fight in front of the children. The wisdom in this lies in the fact that a child needs to feel safe and be able to relax in order to play in a healthy way. In an environment that is charged with negative energy, children are overwhelmed. Some will mimic the shouting and fighting, while others (the more sensitive) will withdraw and become passive. In both cases the ability for healthy imaginative play diminishes and may even disappear.

More extreme situations such as parental divorce or childhood abuse can create longer lasting interference. The child seems to play but when more closely examined, he will tend to repeat over and over the same scenarios which never evolve or metamorphose in the way healthy play does and should. Sometimes these things cannot be avoided but the strains that are imposed on the child should be recognized for what they are.

Imaginitive play is the most important thing that a preschool child can do to develop the tools she needs for later life. Our modern lifestyle, hostage to the machines and technology that support it, seems inadvertently to be endangering many of the rhythms and traditions that make for a healthy childhood. We can hope that the Waldorf approach, and the growing interest that it is generating outside its immediate circles, may help restore the realization that sometimes the simple things work best. The experience in our schools, as well as in an increasing body of research, indicates that it may be difficult to improve upon a simple thing like children's play.

Toys Are Not Us
Escaping from the Maw of Consumerism

Let's start with two questions: When you grew up, in how many rooms of the house were your toys located? In your house today, how many rooms of the house have toys in them?

Your answer to the first question is probably "one or maybe two rooms." Your answer to question two, though, is most likely a resounding "every room in the house!" Heavens, why is this so? What is going on?

One explanation for this change may be that, because many mothers today are not full-time homemakers, housekeeping has deteriorated since the time of our parents and grandparents. Another reason may be the generally more lax attitude of baby-boomers to housekeeping. However, the most compelling explanation is that children today just have many more toys—toys that fill every corner of every room, toys that overflow every toy box that attempts to contain them, toys that spread out like some self-replicating plague!

For the aspiring mindful parent, the questions arise: What effect does this plethora of toys have on my child? Do more toys provide proportionally more outlets for creativity, more stimulation for thinking, or just more plain fun? Or does this superabundance of playthings work against children's healthy development? Does it lay the seed for unhealthy habits with respect to consumerism and waste? Are children being overwhelmed? Is their sense of what is valuable and important in life being skewed?

Manufactured, ready-to-use toys are more present in our lives and in the lives of our children than at any time before in history. This is the result of aggressive product development, advertising, and marketing by large toy companies. These companies are primarily interested in toys that will sell and make a profit, not in toys that will foster the healthy development of children. They are interested in convincing parents and children (the latter being the principle target of their advertising) that "the more toys, the happier the child." Many parents and educators, though, are beginning to question this seemingly benign sales mantra.

Claire Lerner is a childhood development researcher with Zero to Three, an organization that runs preschool educational programs across the country. She maintains that certain types of toys as well as an excess of toys can be harmful. According to Lerner, "[The children] get overwhelmed and cannot concentrate on anything long enough to learn from it." Lerner advises fewer toys for all children and no electronic toys at all for young children.

These conclusions are echoed by Oxford University research psychologist Kathy Silva. Silva has been an outspoken advocate in Great Britain for preschools that—in direct contradiction to the current government policies—emphasize play rather than early academics. Her controversial research (controversial, because it contradicts the current educational policies adopted by the British government) has pointedly revealed that "children who have a less structured early education, based on play and song, are more likely to stay married, to vote, to read newspapers and stay out of prison in later life."

Silva is also concerned about "the complex relationship between children's progress, the types of toys they are given, and the time parents spend with them." In a large-scale study of preschoolers funded by the Economic and Social Research Council, she found that when children "have a large number of toys, there seems to be a distraction element, and when children are distracted they do not learn or play well." Silva also discovered that having fewer toys is associated with less solitary play and more sharing with others.

Silva's research was prompted by the concern that childhood is irrevocably altered by parents lavishing toys, computers, and televisions on their children rather than spending time with them. She is especially critical of all electronic toys, since they restrict creativity and imagination, capacities she terms "the essence of childhood."

Silva summarizes her findings by saying that "children with relatively few toys, whose parents spend more time reading, singing, or playing with them . . . surpass youngsters even from more affluent backgrounds."

Rudolf Steiner was clear about what makes up a desirable environment for a young child. He described the child up to the age of seven as one great "sense-organ" that absorbs or takes in everything from his surroundings, including the sounds, colors, and shapes of the physical environment and the emotions, thoughts, and even the moral qualities of the human being. Since children are susceptible to the subtlest influences, Steiner felt that we need to be very conscious of what we place in and what we allow to be in their environment.

Steiner had ideas about toys that, to parents of today, can seem radical. He objected to toys that are complex and detailed. These he felt limit and stifle the imagination of the young child and are more suitable to the abstract thinking of grown-ups. Some of the play of children involves imitating the work and activities of adults. Other, imaginative, play involves the acting out of stories and fantasies of the children's own devising. In both types of play, children do not need function-specific manufactured toys. They can and will make use of ordinary objects that are on hand. A few cardboard boxes will serve as a bus in which to take a trip; a broom can become a trusty steed; a simple piece of cloth, the curtain for a stage. Using and transforming these common objects in play both exercises and strengthens the child's imagination.

The charming "Waldorf doll"—a simple cloth doll with barely indicated facial features, is an excellent example of an appropriate toy for very young children. The doll is made of natural materials—cotton, wool, and silk—that have subtle rather than garish colors. It is elementary in form, having only a torso and legs, a head with two eyes, and perhaps a thin line of a mouth—which is about all that a small child notices about a human being.

Dolls—and toys in general—that are realistic and detailed can bring the child too early into noticing detail and thus beginning to think abstractly. This abstract thinking, according to Steiner, should develop later in childhood. While the adolescent and the adult need to be fully awake intellectually, the young child "needs not to be." The young child needs to live in the peaceful dreaminess of imaginative pictures. So toys should be simple and few. Steiner held that the child who is allowed to live fully in the world of imagination will, ironically, be better able to develop the capacity for abstract thinking when he or she matures.

A report from the first International Toy Research Conference, held in Sweden in 1976, notes that since the early twentieth century the ideal of appropriate parental behavior has become decreasingly authoritarian and increasingly permissive. With this change has come an expectation that parents be more generous—in terms of gifts and possessions—with their children. These trends, combined with the fast pace of modern life with all its accompanying stresses, have resulted in parents providing children with more and more toys. Unfortunately, many parents buy toys—and, later, televisions, videos, and computers—for their children in order to win personal time for themselves apart from their children and, paradoxically, to assuage their feelings of guilt about not spending enough time with them.

Researcher Edward Melhuish of Birkbeck College in England finds, however, that this parental pattern is counterproductive. His work points out that "the behavior of children is directly affected not by the number and sophistication of their toys but by the amount of time parents devote to reciting them stories, rhymes, and songs." He found that those children who spend the most time in these activities at home "are more cooperative, confident and social." He counters the toy industry's motto about more toys with "the more books, the better."

While toys deeply impact younger children, older children are also vulnerable. The materialism of our culture, manifested in consumerism, the mall culture, and the glossy fantasy worlds of mail order catalogues and internet shopping carts, is ubiquitous and compelling. Happiness and status are presented as related to the amount of stylish and expensive possessions. Parents need to decide consciously and carefully to what degree they and their children will participate in the consumer culture. It is easy to give up the fight when confronted by the intense energies of older children and to leave them at the mercy of the materialistic ethos. To go against the mainstream on this point requires will and resolve. Some families are drawn to a Waldorf community as an island of sanity. They find there spiritual values that are counter to the excessively materialistic values that seem to hold sway almost everywhere else. They seek other families embracing values not driven by television, catalogues, and shopping malls.

An article called "Keeping It Simple" (*Time Magazine*, August 6, 2001) tells the story of Reverend John Omer, rector of a church in Leesburg, Virginia. Reverend Omer recognized that parents in his congregation wanted help in breaking the habit of overindulging their children. As a father of three, Omer knew very well the pressures involved, so he initiated what he jokingly referred to as "an underground resistance movement." He gave workshops in which parents could take stock of their family life and how they celebrate the holidays and then imagine a different, more satisfying picture. Not surprisingly, their aspirations involved less credit card debt and a lot less "stuff." Parents began to set limits on the number and the price of holiday and birthday gifts, whether the gift was purchased by themselves or by friends or relatives. Omer observed that the program was successful because in the workshops parents find—for the first time—legitimacy for their frustration and concerns as well as support in dealing with them.

The *Time* article reported on another program, created by Cornell University, called Seeds of Simplicity, which has resulted in the formation of Simplicity Circles in over one hundred U.S. cities. In these groups, parents share ideas on ways to cut back on material possessions and to promote other values in their families. Jennifer Shields, a parent from Silver Spring, Maryland, decided that on birthday invitations to her child's party, she would ask that guests give only art supplies. Also, she strictly limits media exposure in order to keep her child's gift expectations low.

Other strategies that have emerged from Simplicity Circles include: having "bring no gift" parties with classmates, keeping mail order catalogues for children out of the house to decrease the frenzy around getting gifts, and limiting trips to the mall so that children view shopping as a planned and not an impulsive activity. With older children, parents find it helpful to discuss underlying issues and to involve children in the decision-making about simplification.

A related impulse comes from The Center for New American Values in Takoma Park, Maryland. The Center has an ecological mission and seeks to promote sustainable use of the world's natural resources. It sees the consumption patterns of American society as a major contributor to global problems. North Americans consume and waste a disproportionate percentage of the world's resources and products. We also provide an unfortunate example to people in less developed nations who try to emulate our bad habits. The Center works, therefore, to change current habits of consumerism.

The Center has launched a nationwide awareness campaign related to children and promoting a philosophy of "more fun, less stuff!" According to director Betsy Taylor, "This isn't about unspoiling kids. It's about reclaiming our kids from a toxic commercial culture that has spun out of control." The organization's website (www.newdream.org/campaign) offers the online brochures "Tips for Parenting in a Commercial Culture" and "Simplify the Holidays." These point out that current marketing hurts children's self-esteem and gives them a questionable worldview and set of values. The brochures also assert that providing a superabundance of toys is a first step in developing a later generation of "hyperconsumers." Some of the website's Action Tips include:

- Buy music lessons rather than fancy electronic gadgets.
- Turn off the Discovery Channel and go out and make your own discoveries.
- Remove the brand logos from clothes—your children's and your own. Talk with children about why you are doing this.
- Urge your school board to stop selling overpriced magazine subscriptions, wrapping paper, and candy bars.
- Make children responsible for age-appropriate chores around the house.
- Refuse to buy war toys and Ken and Barbie dolls.
- Teach children to be doers and creators, not shoppers and buyers.
- Teach children money management so they understand what things really cost.

- Respect the idea that there will always be an aspect of "I want" in a child.
- Turn off the TV and show children interesting alternative activities.

Many Waldorf parents are careful about the quality of what they buy for their children. They realize that toys and other possessions can affect a child's development. But the quantity of toys, clothes, sports equipment, and so on, is also important. Too much stuff will distract, confuse, and overwhelm. And for the young child, no amount of things can really replace the love and attention and time of parents.

Older children need to learn about giving love and attention to others, both within the home and outside the circle of family and friends, in ever-widening circles. This unfolding soul-capacity to share and to give needs to be nourished and encouraged, not stifled by a preoccupation with getting and accumulating stuff for oneself.

Because of the overwhelming pressures of commercialism, it is very hard for a parent to suddenly embrace a Shaker philosophy that "it's a gift to be simple" and to resist the intrusion of more and more stuff into the home. Enlisting cooperation and support through a dialogue with family and friends, however, can help a family move from the outwardly driven "Toys R Us" way of life to a more intimate and inwardly spontaneous one that appreciates the simple gifts.

Children and Sports – Finding a Balance

Over the last thirty or forty years, the sanctity and wholesomeness of early childhood has been under attack. Exposure to sex and violence in the media, pressure to achieve early reading, academic, and computer competence, and other factors have produced the "hurried child." Many children today are forced into activities and choices for which, in terms of their physical, emotional, and intellectual development, they are not yet ready. This has happened also in the realm of sports.

In previous generations, most children learned and played games such as baseball, basketball, football and soccer in their neighborhood, playing with children who lived nearby. Parents were involved very little in this. The stay-at-home mothers of the time were there if someone got hurt and to provide cold lemonade for thirsty players.

Today unsupervised local play and sports activity is much less common. In many areas there are concerns about safety. Also, since in many families both parents work, there is no one home to provide safety-net supervision. Hence today children are likely to wind up after school in a supervised aftercare situation or doing some adult-organized and led activity. And the organized activity of choice today is sport. Hence we have the ubiquity of the soccer league, the swim team, the basketball league, and so on, complete with uniforms, team names, scheduled games, championships, coaches, sponsors, and so on.

Organized teams and leagues for youngsters did exist in the past, but they were much less common and supplemented rather than replaced neighborhood play. They were mostly for children who were approaching or had entered into adolescence. Today there is a trend to have younger and younger children take part in organized athletic activities—preschool soccer leagues and swim teams, for example. There is also a tendency to have children specialize in a single sport and to do that sport all year round, rather than just during its particular season. While in some communities the idea that sports for children is wholesome play rather than competition, the current growing emphasis is on achievement and winning. Thus organized sports for children have taken on a disturbing life of its own. Often they do not serve the physical and emotional health of the child and undermine rather than enhance the life of the family.

Stresses on Young Bodies

The growing muscles and bones of young children are not strong enough for the rigorous, repetitive training and practice regimens used by adult athletes. When these regimens are imposed on children, problems arise. Overuse injuries are so common that "pediatric sports medicine" is now a recognized medical specialty. Tendonitis is a very common problem among child athletes. Stress fractures, caused by repeated overtaxing of the bones that are not yet fully calcified, are also very common. To make matters worse, almost a quarter of all children with athletic injuries are—according to a study by the Minnesota Amateur Sports Commission—encouraged by parents and coaches to continue playing.

This compromising of the healthy growth of children's bodies goes on in spite of there being no evidence that starting a child before age eight or nine in any organized team sport gives a lasting advantage. Rather, there is abundant evidence that engaging in adult level sports at a young age carries the risk of long-lasting injuries. Besides, many experts in child development—as well as disinterested common sense—tell us that growing children need to experience a variety of physical activities in order to grow in a balanced way.

Stresses on Families

A child's joining an athletic team has a big impact on the child's and also the family schedule and daily life. Homework, music lessons, and other activities have to be squeezed into a suddenly much more full schedule, and there is little space for free play and time to just relax and unwind. The family dinner hour is often disrupted. A regular and appropriately early bedtime is a common casualty as well. Parents usually find that their chauffeuring duties increase markedly as they are enlisted to drive budding athletes to practices and games. Parents may also spend time (willingly or unwillingly) watching games and practices and waiting in parking lots for their children to be ready to go home.

According to New York child psychiatrist Alvin Rosen, in the past generation structured sports time has doubled, unstructured play time has been cut in half and, the family dinner, that essential ingredient in family life, has declined by a third.

Especially problematic has been the proliferation of so-called "travel teams." These teams provide professional-level coaching and stiffer competition and place greater demands on the child and the family. A travel team may practice twice a week and play another two times a week. Away-games can involve round trips of many hours. Such time demands obviously put a lot of pressure on children, parents, and families.

The travel team entices the child with some talent and interest an accelerated development in the sport and the promise of a better chance to "make the team" at the next level. Most travel teams involve children in the year or two before high school, but in some areas the soccer travel team now involves eight-year-olds concerned about making the ten-year old team. As one soccer mom complained, the whole thing can begin to feel like "an arms race."

Often children in travel teams are encouraged to play the same sport for more than one season. They are told that they will fall behind their peers if they do not play all year around. This full-time involvement puts a lot of emotional pressure on the child. The sport takes on an importance far beyond what a recreational activity should have for a child.

Besides, this narrow focus may prevent the balanced physical development that playing a variety of sports brings. The former professional baseball player, Cal Ripken Jr. has been very critical of all-year-round single sport involvement for young people. He feels that specialization in a single sport before age fifteen has no advantages and may, in fact, cause harm. Ripken himself played three sports through high school and attributes some of his success to this. Through soccer he learned footwork and balance, and basketball gave him explosiveness and quickness. Ripken urges aspiring young baseball players children to "put the glove down" when the baseball season is over.

Early Does not Mean Better

The appearance of "the earlier the better" philosophy in sports training is no surprise. Tiger Woods who began to play golf at age three, the East European world class gymnasts who began training soon after they learned to walk, and other similar examples have convinced many parents that their children will miss out if they do not start early.

Sports history, though, reveals that often it is the late-bloomers, who had to work longer and harder to catch up, who later became stars. The same applies to early and intense ballet training as well. Rudolf Nureyev began formal training at age eleven.

There are several pressures on parents to go along with the trend to early organized athletics. When a child of seven or eight comes home reporting that all her friends are joining soccer league, one feels impelled to join the crowd. Besides, many children need more exercise, and there may be no other readily available opportunities for out-of-school group games. Sports may seem to be the only option.

For some parents the hope for their child of a college athletic scholarship or even a career in professional sports is a factor. However, for children involved in organized sports, the dropout rate before adolescence is alarmingly high and is increasing. A *U.S. News & World Report* article (June 7, 2004) called "Fixing Kids' Sports" reports that seventy percent of children involved in early organized sports drop out.

Even for a child who sticks to a sport, the best motivation to do so is love of the game. The odds of even the talented child profiting from persistence are not great. Dan Dayle, director of the Institute of Sports at the University of Rhode Island, cautions parents' hopes for college scholarship. His research shows that of the 475,000 fourth graders playing organized basketball, only 87,000 were still playing as seniors in high school. Of these, less than 3,000 won scholarships for their first year of college, and only 160 made it to the professional level. In soccer, the odds are much longer because many colleges recruit foreign players. For other sports, there is a similarly large gap between those who aspire to get scholarships and those who get them.

The Waldorf Model

In Waldorf schools, the healthy balanced physical development of the child is emphasized, perhaps moreso than in any other approach to education. From the kindergarten through the elementary grades and high school, the children do activities that develop their fine motor and large motor coordination. Finger games, handwork, outdoor games, eurythmy, Spatial Dynamics, and sports comprise an integrated approach to developing healthy bodies that will be the basis for healthy emotional and intellectual lives. Organized sports are indeed important in the healthy development of the child. Waldorf educators do not oppose organized sports but only counsel that they begin at a particular age and be done in a particular way. Most schools have teams beginning in the sixth or seventh grade and going through high school.

During the first seven years the child lives in a world of fantasy and imagination. As Rudolf Steiner said, "Play is the work of the young child." Free play (both indoors and outdoors) and simple non-competitive games are all that is needed for the child's healthy physical development—assuming of course that the diet is a balanced one based on a variety of whole, natural foods.

At this stage, pushing a structured or competitive activity can be problematic. It can lead to a physical, emotional, and psychological "hardening." The young child's body can start to lose its characteristic softness and flexibility. Aggressiveness and competitiveness may develop along with an awakened self-consciousness that is not really appropriate at this stage. Free play and playing non-competitive games for the fun of it should dominate in the first several years of formal school.

After age nine, the child becomes less dreamy, more self-aware and more independent. Also, she begins to be able to really practice, develop, and master the skills involved in a sport such as gymnastics or baseball. She may be ready for organized sports.

If the child does begin an organized athletic activity, the joy of the game rather than competitive achievement should be emphasized. Also, the activity should not become too much of a focus in a child's life. There should be other activities and other sports. A healthy family life should continue to be a priority. If a sports involvement is wreaking havoc with a family's daily schedule and with their time together, that involvement should be critically examined.

Even if the child shows interest and promise in a sport, it is best to proceed slowly. Travel teams, four days a week of gymnastic practice and the like are best left until the child is a few years older.

Some parents fall into the trap of over-scheduling their child, of arranging too many activities. Some parents enroll their children in two or more sports in a single season, while arranging a smorgasbord of sports, art, and other activities. Children need lots of unstructured time to relax and do what comes to mind. For the younger child, over-scheduling may lead to health and emotional distress. Even after age twelve the young person needs unscheduled free time.

For teenagers, sports and physical activity are very important. They tend to have a surplus of energy that needs to be channeled. When those energies can find no focus, the three temptations of "sex, drugs and rock and roll" become overly seductive and the dangers of teenage depression and obesity rear up. Sports and physical disciplines such as dance, eurythmy, and martial arts, as well as drama and music are ideal at this time. Unfortunately, with the current emphasis on early sports, many young people are burnt out by the time they reach high school. Having played a hundred soccer games a year before they set foot in high school, they are ready to take a rest. The high dropout rate in youth sports means that when young people really need this outlet in their adolescent years, many have already given up on it.

The American Academy of Pediatrics released the following statement in 2000:

Those who participate in a variety of sports and specialize only after reaching puberty tend to be more consistent performers, have fewer injuries and adhere to sports play longer than those who specialize early.

In many areas of modern life, the adult world is impinging on the world of childhood. With the "ratings creep" in movies, for example, adult content and language are increasingly allowed in G- and PG-rated films. This is happening in the world of sport as well.

Parents and teachers need to work together to see that children are protected from the very problematic trend of intense, early athletic competition. Waldorf educators generally have a clear idea of what is appropriate for the children in their classes. It is up to parents to sees that outside school hours their children and their family life are not adversely affected by current trends in intense, early organized sports activities. Parents of younger children can arrange children's play and sports gatherings outside the local league system. If there is no local neighborhood, parents can recreate an "intentional neighborhood" to do the same. Children need only to be brought together in a safe venue, given the necessary equipment, have the rules explained, and then be left pretty much to themselves. A weekly after-school second grade baseball get-together, for example, can be an alternative to the more intense organized league.

When a child is ready for organized sports, the parent can ensure that it does not adversely affect the child or family life. Sports can provide young people with enjoyable and valuable experiences. Sports is an important part of life, but only a part.

Etheric? Astral? Ego?

An Esoteric View of the Human Being and Its Value in the Education of the Child

Rachel Resnick was looking for a good private school for her child. She did a research tour of the private schools in her area: the Montessori, the Solomon Schechter, the lab school of a prestigious local college, the alternative "free" school, and a Waldorf school. She wound up visiting the local Waldorf school three times and, in the end, remarked to a teacher there, "This is the only real alternative school [I've seen]," and wanted to understand what was behind this difference.

It is not easy to present the worldview behind Waldorf education that makes it so different. One could begin by saying that Rudolf Steiner perceived the child as a spiritual being, not merely as a "higher animal" that needs to be trained or a supercomputer whose brain needs to be properly programmed. One would have to present in more detail the "nonvisible" aspects of the child, how they relate to the physical body, how Waldorf education takes each of these aspects of the child into consideration, and how it tries to develop each in a healthy manner.

Body, Soul, and Spirit

The understanding that the human being consists of a body, a soul, and a spirit is an ancient and almost universal one. Some religious and philosophical systems see the physical body as consisting of two parts—a material, physical body and a nonmaterial, etheric or life body. Add soul and spirit, and we have the fourfold picture of the human being that has been recognized for centuries by various cultures. Steiner sometimes used the Sanskrit terms of ancient India to denote these four dimensions, but more often employed the theosophical terms current in his day—physical body, etheric body, astral body (for the realm of soul), and the I (for the spirit component).

The physical body, which consists of chemical elements and which has weight and dimension, is that part of the human being that we perceive most readily with our physical senses. It can be seen, felt, smelled, and so on. In ancient India it was called the *annamaya kosha*, or "body made of food." In the past century, Western mainstream medicine has focused almost exclusively on the physical body. This was not the case earlier in the West nor has it ever been the case in non-Western countries. Among the kingdoms of nature, only the minerals have just a physical body.

The etheric body gives form and life to the physical body. The ancient Indian Hindus called it the *pranamaya kosha*, or "body made of vital energy (*prana*)." The etheric body is the source of all health and vitality. Its forces build up and shape the human body, cause it to grow, and repair it when it is injured or sick. The etheric body is called *chi* in China and *ki* in Japan and is utilized in Eastern medicine and martial arts. For the most part dismissed as a superstition by Western science, the etheric body is gradually coming to be recognized as a real part of the human being. Alternative therapies such as acupuncture and reiki utilize the life-bearing etheric forces in the service of healing. At death, the etheric body separates from the physical body, and the latter, bereft of its life-giving forces, decomposes. Plants have etheric bodies as well as physical bodies and thus are distinct from minerals.

The astral or "star" body (or what we call the "soul") endows the human being with the ability to move, as well as instinct and a basic kind of thinking and consciousness. The ancient Indians used the term *manomaya kosha*, or "body made of thought." Our feelings, thoughts, impulses of will, likes and dislikes, agonies and ecstasies, our normal waking consciousness—all are activities of the astral body. Often a complex maelstrom, a locus of tempest and passion, the astral body is the province of psychologists, poets, and priests. But it may also be characterized by calm awakeness and clear consciousness. Animals also have an astral body, though one much less complex than that of human beings.

The I is the spiritual core of the human being, that which sets us apart from the animals. The Latin term *ego* is problematic because psychologists and philosophers have used the word in many different ways. The I is the eternal individuality, the spiritual being who inhabits our other three bodies. This eternal I is pure and free of "egoism"—which is rather an aspect of the desirous astral body. The I represents the objective judge within us, the source of discernment, insight, and conscience. It is the center of strength that maintains us through adversity. The needs and desires of the self-centered astral body are constantly diverting us from an experience of the I and occupy most of our waking experience. Meditation and religious practice seek to make us more sensitive and responsive to the guidance of the I. The I can be understood as "pure attention," and its activity as "mindfulness." The various religious traditions understand the destiny of the I in various ways. According to some traditions, after death the I goes to heaven or hell, depending on how well the human being has lived. According to others, the I is later reincarnated in another human body.

The Three Seven-Year Stages

At birth an infant possesses all four bodies, but each is not yet "unfolded." In the years before adulthood, each of the bodies develops according to a basic pattern.

Unlike Pallas Athena, who emerged from the head of Zeus fully mature and clothed in a suit of armor, children experience a slow and gradual incarnation of their four bodies. At birth, the physical body comes into the world and grows very rapidly. Most of the energy and resources of the child go into supporting this physical growth. This first stage lasts for about seven years. A second seven-year period brings the child to puberty, and a third to adulthood at about the age of twenty-one.

At birth the physical body of the infant is freed from that of the mother. The other bodies, though, are not yet so independent. The etheric body of the mother is intermingled with that of the child and surrounds and protects it. Within this second womb, the amazingly rapid and complicated process of physical growth takes place. During this period, although the child is physically separate from the mother, their etheric connection is such that the mother's life forces continue to influence the child. This connection weakens as the child grows older and more independent.

When the child is around seven years old, the life forces undertake the emergence of the second teeth, the densest and hardest part of the physical body. This sign heralds a kind of second birth. The etheric body of the child is now independent from that of the mother. Also, the child's etheric body need no longer be totally involved in the growth of the physical body. It is freed to help in the development of important human capacities, particularly those of memory and thinking.

It is for this reason that in Waldorf education intellectual, academic work begins only after age seven. The younger child can often do such work earlier, but the life forces that are needed for the complex work of building up the physical body will be diverted from their main task, and the healthy development of the physical body may be compromised. Premature academic work can also lead to a loss of interest in and enthusiasm for learning. Some children are unable to do the work (because they are in fact not ready for it) and may experience feelings of inferiority. The phenomenon of "school sickness," the refusal of young children to go to school, can result from this demand for early academic performance.

In the second period of seven years, the child is ready for academic learning. A true "declaration of independence" by the child usually occurs a couple of years later, around the age of nine. In this so-called nine-year change, the child experiences for the first time a clear sense of its separate identity vis-à-vis the world and other human beings. Some of the dreaminess of early childhood is replaced by a more awake (often startlingly so) confrontation with the world—including the adults surrounding the child!

During the second seven-year period, the child is enclosed in another protective envelope, the astral or "feeling-life" womb. While the etheric womb of the first seven years is provided primarily by the mother, the astral womb is the product of the emotional and moral life of all the adults around the child. This is the basis of the maxim, "It takes a village to raise a child." During these years the child still needs protection of her life forces. What is crucial now, however, is emotional protection from being exposed too soon to the realities of adult life.

The third seven-year period (from age fourteen to age twenty-one) is the period of adolescence whose onset is marked by puberty, the changing of the voice, and the development of clear sexual characteristics. This is the time when the astral body of the human being develops. David Elkind, well-known author of *The Hurried Child* and other books, maintains that today's preadolescent children are being pushed prematurely into the world of the adolescent. They meet emotional challenges which they are too young to handle and are being robbed of their very childhood. This can lead to later problems, primarily in the realms of relationships, sex, and drug and alcohol use.

Between ages seven and fourteen, the child should be allowed to mature and develop at an unpressured pace, particularly in his feeling life. For this the child needs to be protected, held, and directed by his parents and teachers in their roles as loving but firm authority figures. The child will then feel safe to experiment in a playful and innocent fashion, instead of being thrust too early into the more complex and confusing realm of grownup love and hate, the extremes of agony and ecstasy and trauma. Media and commercialism are the most common culprits in stealing the innocence of children in stable families. In broken families, the children are afflicted as well by parental tensions and conflicts. Too early an exposure to these influences and experiences can desensitize the child and maim his or her later ability to tackle the complex issues of human relationships with equanimity and common sense.

With the onset of adolescence, the feeling nature is released from the physical and etheric bodies and gradually becomes able to deal with the challenges of a more complicated emotional and social life. Parents and other adults around the child need to slowly relinquish the often uncomfortable role of authority figure that they have played. Virtually all traditional cultures have recognized the spiritual reality of the maturation of the child's astral body and have marked this in "coming of age" ceremonies. While these have largely disappeared in our culture, the Jewish bar mitzvah and Hispanic "sweet sixteen" celebrations are remnants of this tradition.

Not until age twenty-one, though, is the individual fully accepted as an adult. At about this age the I, or spiritual ego, finally incarnates, though in fact the process may take two or three years to be complete. The right to vote was for many years reserved for this time when a more objective capacity for judgment was recognized. In many states, the right to drink alcohol, a substance that displaces the ego, is also associated with this level of maturity.

Caring for the Rhythms of Life

This picture of the gradual incarnation of the child is one of the bases for the effectiveness of Waldorf education. It gives Waldorf educators a deep understanding of what children really need at each stage of their development. Nursery and kindergarten teachers and class teachers in the first three grades, for example, are acutely aware of the importance of the child's etheric body. While some rare individuals can actually see these forces (the healer and author of *Hands of Light*, Barbara Brennan, is apparently one such person), for most of us, close observation, some training, and native intuition provide sufficient sensitivity.

The etheric or life-formative body can be characterized as warm and as pulsing with a calm, steady rhythm—something like a large human heart. It is just these qualities that we seek to provide for younger children. We must surround our children with warmth, both physical and emotional. Sometimes we need to struggle with them to put on their wool hats and extra sweaters. At other times we need to impose an extra layer of parental protection. A cozy and protected nest created at home and at school conserves and strengthens the child's etheric forces.

Rhythm in daily life is the other factor crucial for the well-being of the etheric body. The major rhythms that need to be developed and maintained for the child are those of mealtimes and bedtime. Children should have their meals and should go to bed at roughly the same time all seven days of the week (though holiday times may invite some flexibility).

Establishing this regular daily rhythm can be difficult for parents. As adults we are much more under the influence of our own astral nature and its wants, desires, and emotional ups and downs. Our desire to be somewhere else and to be doing something else and our desire to be spontaneous and undisciplined will often conflict with maintaining a regular schedule for our children. But part of being a parent is sacrificing one's own interests for the sake of one's children. And the vagaries of the adult's astral do nothing but disrupt the needs of the child's etheric body. The child's rhythms are like those of the moon and the tides and, if supported by external rhythms, will hum along quietly and smoothly. What upsets and weakens the etheric body are the astral tempests and the accompanying disruptions of daily rhythms. The effect is passed on to the physical body. The endocrine balance is upset, adrenaline is released, and the breath and the circulation of blood are disturbed.

A challenge, especially for younger parents who themselves enjoy a more active life, is to protect their children from overstimulation, particularly before the age of nine. Among the things that adults take for granted but that can overtax the child are:

- travel and visiting new places
- time spent in automobiles
- literature meant for older children (Harry Potter, et al.)
- crowded places such as supermarkets, department stores, sporting events, roller coasters and other amusements that depend on fear and excitement
- participation in competitive sports
- rock, hip-hop, rap, and other music meant for adults
- radio, television shows, movies, DVDs, and computer games that are meant for pre-teens and adolescents, not for young children

All of these influences—like the rock music that, played in a greenhouse, causes the plants to shrivel and die—will weaken and dissipate a child's life forces.

A good deal of discipline and self-sacrifice are required to provide this ethetically calm and protected space for a family. The desired mood can be compared to a cow's slow, even munching of grass. To persons of even temperament, this may not be difficult. For others, it will require conscious effort and the changing of established habits. The etheric body needs predictability, evenness, and lots of rest. To provide this for their children, parents themselves need to slow down and, often, stay home or close to home a lot more. They need to carefully plan transitions from one activity to another so that they and their children will not be rushed and pressured. And they need to avoid emotional outbursts when with the children.

A wholesome diet, rather than one based on fast food and snacks, is also important. Fat is a nutrient that is most essential to the etheric body, and children should get a variety of high quality fats and oils from both animal and vegetable sources. The favorite food of children today is French fries, but oil that has been heated to high temperatures is not so desirable. Especially important are the so-called "essential fatty acids" available most plentifully in oil-rich fish, but also in egg yolks and seeds (including flax seeds and nuts, particularly walnuts). Parents should have care when imposing their own low-fat, vegan, or vegetarian diets on their children. Such restricted regimens can harm children physically and emotionally.

Some forms of attention deficit and hyperactivity syndromes respond to a therapy focusing exclusively on extra care for the etheric body of the child. This involves an improved diet that includes omega-3 essential fatty acids, the establishing and maintaining of a clear rhythm of daily and weekly family life, and setting and enforcing firm, clear limits on behavior. In order to grow and thrive, these children need a clear and predictable environment in which they can feel safe.

When a child's etheric body is not getting the care and protection it needs, the signs can include irritability, dark circles under the eyes, poor appetite, being easily agitated or overly tired, and a pale, sallow complexion. Frequent illness can also be a symptom of etheric draining. A quiet and calm home atmosphere, a clear, regular daily rhythm of life, the exclusion of junk food and of the junk stimulation of television and other electronic media, and the loving attention of grounded adults together comprise "chicken soup for the ether body." These measures can revive and strengthen the life forces in a child and, in doing so, can restore a healthy blush to well-rounded cheeks.

For the older child, it is the unfolding soul that needs protecting. A child of ten, or even of thirteen, is not ready to deal with the world of "drugs, sex, and rock and roll," though in many instances this world may have already been thrust upon her. The attention and vigilance required of parents to create this protection for children and early teenage children is great and also time-consuming. Parents must stand not only as role models but as authority figures in providing guidance to their children. Being an authority figure does not mean being authoritarian. Parents need to stay interested in what their children are interested in and maintain an active dialogue with them and their friends. But parents need to recognize that their primary role is not to be their child's buddy, but rather to be a source of higher judgment that sets reasonable standards of behavior and follows through to see that they are observed.

In considering influences on our children's evolving soul life, we have to decide what we want to keep out and what we want to encourage. The list of things to exclude includes adult and adolescent clothing and fashions—particularly sexually suggestive attire, tattoos, body jewelry, and so on. These are obvious, but we also need to be aware of anything that is too stimulating—garish pictures of monsters and of bizarre machines, for example, and other "in-your-face" images. All forms of media need to be monitored, not just for surface content of sex, violence, and crude language, but also for their intensity or pacing. In Japan a few years back, the succession of images in a children's television program was so frenetic that it caused seizures in hundreds of children. Other research has shown that exposure to video games resets the threshold of pleasure in children so that everything else is boring to them—especially school.

The aim here is to help children retain the innocence and wholesomeness of childhood, to delay their encounter with adolescent "cool" until they are truly adolescents. Parents can effectively act as guardians at the threshold of the adult world. Other practical steps include: putting off the time when a child has a personal radio or stereo, not allowing a television or computer in the child's room (otherwise, content and amount of use cannot be monitored), limiting television and video viewing, watching with your child when he does watch (so you can serve as a moderating influence), and being firm about his seeing only movies that are appropriate for his age.

On the other hand, we want to promote those things that enrich our children's feeling life and create in them an appreciation for what is true, beautiful, and good. Waldorf education works toward this goal consciously, but support at home is vital. Encounters with nature and cultivation of the arts should be a regular part of family life. Individual music lessons (in addition to the group lessons at school) are an effective character builder. Too much sports and too intensive training while a child is still young are also problems (see the chapter on "Children and Sports").

The experience and habit of serving and of caring for others can begin with children having regular chores at home—for which they are not paid! Taking care of pets is also an excellent step in this direction. Older children can be given the experience of caring for the young, the sick, the elderly, the disabled, and the poor.

Finally, each family needs a clear set of behavioral and moral standards that are made explicit, that are taught to the children, and that are modeled by the adults. Manners, civility, consideration of others, truthfulness and honesty, the treatment of all family members, friends, acquaintances, and strangers with respect, and speech that is civil and free of profanity are all part of this. There is a coarsening today in speech, behavior, and morals that can be redeemed only by conscious and concerted efforts within each family.

Religious instruction and practice can also be important for a child, even if the parents themselves are not motivated in this direction. One antidote to the dubious offerings of popular culture is the cultivation of a sense of wonder and magic in childhood. The noted Jewish commentator on family and religious issues, Rabbi Harold Kushner, maintains that, for children, being taken to church or synagogue, experiencing the beauty of the sacred space—the light streaming through stained glass windows—and of the ritual, and taking part in the service foster an expansion of the child's being. They prepare the child to appreciate a level of reality that is unseen, that is not just about buying and having.

The celebration of seasonal rituals also promotes the development of this spiritual sensitivity. The predictable rhythm of these events itself is nourishment for the child's etheric body. Even the young child will sense that something very pure and important is going on. The child's active participation in the ritual starts to empower the nascent astral body.

When the child reaches adolescence at about the age of fourteen, the astral body or soul is now ready to experiment in the world with a greater degree of independence, to learn by trial and error, and to accept the consequences of these experiments. Teenagers still lack a fully present ego or I to guide them in an objective, balanced way. That is why they still need adults near at hand. Parents have to learn the intricate dance of moving in and out of their children's lives, allowing a measure of freedom, and then reasserting their authority as needed—and seldom getting the timing just right. Teenagers need space but they also need extremely vigilant parents.

It is ideal if a teenager has one or two major, wholesome interests (playing a sport, horseback riding, playing a musical instrument, repairing old automobiles, collecting stamps, and the like) into which abundant adolescent energies can be channeled. A physical activity or sport is good, because it can be an efficient outlet in the moment as well as become a healthful lifelong activity. If an adolescent is unable to find a focus, the excess energy can lead to behavioral and/or emotional problems. But extracurricular activities should not be overdone. Moderation and balance between activity and relaxation is as important here as in the other stages of childhood. Too many lessons, too many sports, and too many hours of part-time work have their own dangers. The topic of adolescence warrants much more discussion, but we must save that for another article.

That a human being consists of four bodies (one of which is physical and three of which are spiritual) is an ancient truth that has for the most part been set aside over the past century. It is, however, a concept that can be grasped and applied in our work with children. For parents, an understanding of how these four bodies manifest in the child's development can be a source of guidance throughout a child's growing up.

Sheltering and promoting the unfolding of these physical and spiritual bodies in the right way requires the parent to acquire a new perspective, new sensitivities, and new ways of doing things. Life today in our highly technological, commercially-oriented society is largely antagonistic to a child- and family-centered way of life. Still less does it pretend to honor anything so delicate as the unfolding of the etheric and astral bodies. Raising a child with these concerns in mind and in the midst of economic and societal pressures is a daunting task. It is not possible to do a perfect job of meeting all the subtle needs of the child, and it may not be advisable even to try. Again moderation and balance are key.

Fortunately, raising a child is not an exact science. There is a built-in forgiveness factor and hence some room for flexibility. Make more time for your children, especially as they grow older. Take frequent looks at your family and its life together. Ask whether you meet your own standards of civility, of morals, of spirituality. Finally, protect your children from losing their childhood prematurely—neither you nor they will regret it.

Paradise Lost: The Nine-Year Change

Matthew was a angel as a young child—sensitive, well-behaved, affectionate, often joyful, and often dreaming away on another plane. After turning nine, however, he soon changed into quite a different person. He was sometimes rude and critical, and often very moody if not downright wretched. He had definitely come crashing down to earth, but what a rude awakening for those around him!

Child development specialists have long recognized that between age nine and ten children undergo a marked change. Some experts describe this transition as the crossing of the dividing line between early childhood and full childhood, while others speak in more romantic terms of a "fall from grace." The psychologist Louise Bates Ames has written a series of parent guides describing each year of child development. While her book on the eight-year old bears the subtitle "Lively & Outgoing," the book on age nine bears the more somber "Thoughtful & Mysterious" as its subtitle. So what is it that is going on?

Almost a century ago, Rudolf Steiner studied the developmental stages of childhood. He identified three seven-year stages in the child's passage from birth to adulthood. At birth the child emerges as an independent physical being in the world. But according to Steiner, the unique individuality or ego of the child incarnates or takes hold of this body only gradually. In each of the seven year stages, the ego manifests itself more fully.

The first glimmer of this individuality occurs when the child turns two. Taking place partway through the first seven-year period (birth to age seven), this stage of development is commonly known as "the terrible twos"! What makes this time terrible is that the child is making his first concerted effort to be recognized as a separate person. An important milestone in this process occurs when, usually around the third birthday, the child begins to use the word "I" and to really understand what the word means.

The second seven-year period (age seven through fourteen) is also marked by a significant watershed after the second year. This is "the nine-year change" or "nine-year crisis," that Matthew experienced. It is a confusing transition for child and parents that may involve moments of crisis that are a preview of things to come during adolescence.

In the third seven-year period—fourteen through twenty-one—there is another important milestone, also after the end of the second year. Around the sixteenth birthday, the adolescent begins to manifest a deeper sense of self and a fuller maturity. This fuller incarnation of the ego is acknowledged in the tradition of sweet sixteen celebrations for girls and in giving sixteen-year-olds the right to learn to drive an automobile, to work, and to leave school if they wish.

Prior to age seven or eight, most children are sunny, smiling, exuberant, joyful beings—little angels, for the most part. Around the ninth birthday, however, a tinge of melancholy and self-consciousness begins to creep in. Up to this time, the child has lived and learned through imitation, taking in the world around and echoing its moods and its patterns. Now, though, the harmonious resonance between child and world quickly fades. The child begins to separate from the world and finds herself standing apart and alone.

This shift in the experience of self and world is, of course, difficult for the child. In developing Waldorf education, Steiner tried to help children deal with this experience. Thus in the third grade, Waldorf children learn the story of Adam and Eve and the expulsion from the Garden of Eden. Also, in most Waldorf schools, there is during the Christmas season a performance by adults in the community of "The Paradise Play," a medieval play that vividly depicts this same story of the loss of innocence and the leaving of Paradise. The children are allowed to watch this play only after they have entered the third grade. The story of Adam and Eve is meaningful for nine-year-olds because they are going through their own inner expulsion from Paradise.

Billy Collins, a Poet Laureate of the United States, poignantly captures the essence of this age in a poem called "On Turning Ten":

> *The whole idea makes me feel*
> *like I'm coming down with something,*
> *something worse than any stomach ache*
> *or the headaches I get from reading in bad light—*
> *a kind of measles of the spirit,*
> *a mumps of the psyche,*
> *a disfiguring chicken pox of the soul.*
>
> *You tell me it is too early to be looking back,*
> *but that is because you have forgotten*
> *the perfect simplicity of being one*
> *and the beautiful complexity introduced by two.*
> *But I can lie on my bed and remember every digit.*
> *At four I was an Arabian wizard.*
> *I could make myself invisible*
> *by drinking a glass of milk a certain way.*
> *At seven I was a soldier, at nine a prince.*

But now I am mostly at the window
watching the late afternoon light.
Back then it never fell so solemnly
against the side of my tree house,
and my bicycle never leaned against the garage
as it does today,
all the dark blue speed drained out of it.

This is the beginning of sadness, I say to myself,
as I walk through the universe in my sneakers.
It is time to say good-bye to my imaginary friends,
time to turn the first big number.
It seems only yesterday I used to believe
there was nothing under my skin but light.
If you cut me I would shine.
But now when I fall upon the sidewalks of life,
I skin my knees. I bleed.

This is a time of irritability and unsureness, of trepidation and aloneness. The young child's experience of being part of the world vanishes and she now must learn to stand on her own. The eidetic or photographic memory of early childhood usually disappears and the child needs to learn to memorize. Emotionally, the child experiences a withdrawal into the self for perhaps the first time, a shutting out of the outside world.

The nine-year-old child can feel constrained by both space and time. Like the adolescent, the child now wants more independence and privacy. The nine-year-old may begin wanting his own room or private play space if he does not already have that. He especially needs space from siblings to read or to just think—or to stare out at the late afternoon light. This new desire for privacy and solitude can be unsettling for the parent: "My little baby is becoming a stranger with an inner, private life of which I cannot be part!"

The nine-year-old typically likes to plan her days and to know what is coming ahead of time. She also feels pressured and anxious about getting done all that she has to do. Now there are chores, music practice, homework, after school lessons, and sports. The parent needs to respect the nine-year-old's continuing need for non-organized time for play and for just dreaming. Wise parents teach their children, by word and by example, to take one thing at a time and to undertake only what they can comfortably manage. Parents may even take the initiative to limit a child's activities.

The nine-year-old child is yearning for autonomy, but parental warmth, affection, and support continue to be important. Though the child can be irritable and seems to want to push away, he still needs hugs and comforting from the adults around him. A nine-year-old will sometimes hover near a parent wanting and waiting for a reassuring hug, but hesitant to ask for it. A child will sometimes be more prickly and hyper-sensitive with one parent more than the other, this being affected by the respective temperaments of child and parents. Sometimes one parent needs to step back and let the other be more involved with the child.

Many children have some psychosomatic symptoms around this time. Heart palpitations, breathing problems and headaches are not unusual. Nine-year-olds tend to be worriers and some physical symptoms may be related to that. Nightmares—dreams of being chased or being bitten by a snake or even of being murdered—are common and no reason for great concern. Dreams of storms and runaway fires are also frequent.

For the nine-year-old, suddenly cut off from the world, forced to stand on her own, and beset perhaps by physical problems, anxiety is a dominant emotion. Hence, the child depends on the structure and guidance that watchful adults can give to provide stability and a sense of security. The child needs the solid authority of teachers and a firm parental presence. Otherwise she will be overwhelmed by a sense of insecurity.

The nine-year-old likes to have rules. Adults need to be fair and consistent in enforcing them, however. Fairness is important for the nine-year-old. Though sensitive to being corrected, the child will accept remonstration and even punishment if it seems just and if blame is shared by all responsible. That is because, along with his greater self sufficiency, the nine-year-old is developing a conscience, an internal arbiter of what is right and what is wrong. He recognizes when he has failed to do right and will even confess a wrong-doing to adults because of an uneasy conscience. The nine-year-old expects honesty, fairness and truthfulness from others—and from himself.

Usually during the ninth year, the child begins to reflect on issues such as evil and death. The fairy tales heard at an earlier age have helped prepare the child for meeting the world and its realities. But now the dreamy young child is much more awake and conscious and it is a fairy tale no longer. In grappling with these newly-serious issues, the child experiences that she has something or someone inside that can stand up to these frightening external realities. Some parents change the bedtime prayer at this point to help with the new challenges the child is encountering. When my own two sons were very young, my wife and I used a very simple verse that emphasized protection:

When I go to sleep at night
An angel watches over me
And fills my soul with flooding light
And guides me to the stars so bright
And blesses me each morning…

After our older son turned nine, we switched to something more complex, stressing uprightness and connection to others:

From my head to my feet, I am the image of God.
From my heart to my hands, His own breath do I feel.
When I speak with my mouth, I follow God's will.
When I behold God everywhere, in mother and father,
In all dear people,
In beast and in flower, in tree and in stone,
Nothing brings fear, but love to all that is around me…

Though nine-year-olds may lose the interest in religion they had as eight-year-olds and may not want to go to church or Sunday School, they will pray.

The Waldorf curriculum seeks to help the child in dealing with these challenges. In the third grade, when most of the children are early in the nine-year change and are interested in hearing about people's connection to God, they learn stories from the Old Testament. The fourth grade curriculum provides a quite different experience with the study of the Norse myths. In these, the gods—like the children themselves and also their parents and teachers—have weaknesses, flaws, and moral lapses, and can be criticized. These stories give the children the imagination that they are brave warriors who must struggle against adverse conditions. The children live with images of the mighty Thor battling with his hammer and Vulcan beating iron at his forge. In speech exercises and in eurythmy class, the students stamp their feet to alliterative verses such as, "I war with the wind, with the waves I wrestle. . ." In many schools, the children engage in outdoor adventure activities during the fourth grade, activities that challenge them to overcome fears and limitations. Also, the introduction of homework indicates to the child that the time has come for more serious things.

The changes that children undergo between ages nine and ten can be confusing and challenging for parents and teachers as well as for the children themselves. We adults need to be aware that these changes represent a necessary stage in the development of the child and that they do not go on forever. Also, we need to provide love, support, and guidance to our children during this transitional time of inwardness and loneliness. And we need to be ready to let go of our "little angels" and accept them as unfolding young men and women in the making. In the end, this stage will lead to a new self assurance and sense of independence and identity in the child.

The fourth grade eurythmy classes often do a verse in movement based on the five-pointed star. As the child experiences himself as this star, with two arms, two legs and head as the five points, the verse by Steiner expresses the self-empowerment that is the ideal for the next stage of childhood:

Steadfast I'll stand in the world,
With certainty I'll tread the path of life,
Love I'll cherish in the depths of my being,
Hope shall be in all my doing,
Confidence I'll impress into my thinking.

The Four Temperaments

One of the many surprises for parents new to Waldorf education comes when they hear their child referred to in some seemingly arcane terminology: "You see Mr. and Mrs. Smith, your daughter's real problem is that she is overly phlegmatic."

Goodness, what to make of that! The teacher is not identifying a contagious or terminal condition, only describing the child in terms of the theory of the temperaments. Let us look at the history of this theory, the characteristics of each of the four temperaments—melancholic, phlegmatic, sanguine, and choleric—and how we can use this understanding of human types to help our children develop into well-balanced individuals.

The Temperaments in Premodern Thought

The notion of temperament is very old, dating back at least to the ancient Greece. Hippocrates, in the fourth century BC, spoke of four qualities or "humors" in the human being—cold, moist, hot and dry. In the second century AD, the physician, Galen, spoke of the mixing or "temperare" of these four humors to yield four temperaments. These in turn were related to the four elements yielding the fiery choleric, the airy sanguine, the watery phlegmatic, and the earthy melancholic.

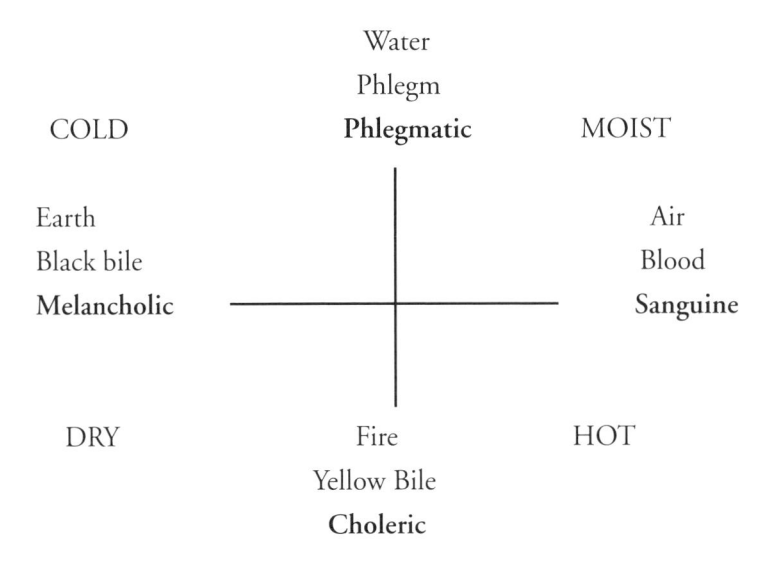

```
                    Water
                    Phlegm
COLD              Phlegmatic        MOIST
                       |
  Earth                |               Air
  Black bile           |               Blood
  Melancholic  ————————+————————    Sanguine
                       |
                       |
  DRY                 Fire           HOT
                   Yellow Bile
                    Choleric
```

    The Greeks sought to explain temperament as being due to an excess of inner fluids. Thus there arose the theory that the melancholic was cool and dry (as often perceived when you hold their hand) due to an excess of black bile. Similarly, was the sanguine warm and moist due to too much blood, the choleric character due to an excess of yellow bile, and the phlegmatic to too much phlegm. At least this is the medieval reading of the Greeks attribution of temperament to biles—it may be that these were terms used in the Greek Mysteries to represent spiritual phenomena which some ten centuries later was interpreted by the uninitiated in a purely materialistic matter. Alas, one of the barriers to the acceptance of these temperaments in this century was the dubiousness of connecting temperament to these fluids. What is black bile, anyway?

Nevertheless, the concept of temperament remained important and widely used in understanding human character and behavior until the Enlightenment. With the development of psychology in the late nineteenth century, the idea that a child's upbringing is the primary determinant of personality and character became the academic orthodoxy. By the beginning of the twentieth century, the notion of temperament was "exiled" because it became politically incorrect to speak of inborn qualities of human beings. The theory of genetic inferiority arose in America with the inflow of poor and uneducated immigrants from eastern and southern Europe and in Germany with the Nazi writings on the superiority of the Aryan race. All this made the study of inborn or temperamental factors taboo.

Modern Science Discovers the Temperaments

In the 1950s several researchers in psychology (among them Stella Chess and Alexander Thomas) began to re-explore the concept of temperament. Initially they were spurred by Carl Jung's concept of introvert-extrovert (and the later Myers-Briggs research on personality types) and by studies that showed that stable and loving parents can still have aggressive or excessively fearful children for which no psychological cause could be found. Thus researchers began to look at the stable qualities which exist in the young child and continue into adulthood, the most prominent among these being inhibited and uninhibited behaviors.

In his book *Galen's Prophecy* (Basic Books, 1994), research psychologist Jerome Kagan describes how he and his colleagues found that inhibited children begin to show indications of their temperament after their first birthday, reacting to new events with initial caution and hesitation. These children tend to withdraw or fret when faced with the unfamiliar and cling to their mothers in the presence of strangers. It was found that twenty percent of healthy infants are thus easily aroused by new experiences and when aroused, become distressed. Most of these later become fearful, cautious children.

The study showed that uninhibited children in contrast are hard to frighten. They take going to school for the first time in stride. They laugh easily and are socially confident and relaxed. This group, who grow up to be bold, outgoing, and socially unflappable adults, comprise about fifteen percent of all children.

Associating body type with personality is an important part of the outmoded —in the eyes of science, at least—theory of temperaments. It is interesting then that data collected supported a connection between temperament and body type. This correlation was initially shocking and resisted by the researchers because it contradicted current assumptions in the field.

Kagan and his colleagues found that inhibited children tend to have slim bodies, narrow faces, and a proneness to allergies and constipation. A significant number have light blue eyes (which alarmed them further due to possible racial implications) and greater than average heart-rate activity. A slight majority are females. Among the uninhibited children, the majority are boys, especially the boldest and most active in the group. They tend to be stockily-built with broad faces, and sixty percent have dark eyes. Some, however, are slim; the key physical marker in children apparently is a stronger musculature around the base of the neck.

These physical characteristics of temperament led Kagan to wonder about differences in the brain and in levels of responsiveness in the nervous system. He found that the two types differed in terms of the threshold of excitability of the grey mass at the base of the brain, the amygdala, and of its projections into the sympathetic nervous system. This "hardwiring," however, did not imply that there was no hope for the children with the most extreme symptoms of temperament— most became either less fearful or less aggressive and ebullient and more to the middle range as they got older. Researchers have now become interested in how they might help this process of modifying temperamental extremes although this work is still exploratory. The main import of this research for the parent and teacher is that some children have temperamental tendencies that are not due to parental upbringing or entirely linked to heredity.

Modern researchers such as Kagan identified the melancholic or inhibited child and the choleric or uninhibited child but failed to distinguish the other two temperaments of the sanguine and phlegmatic. Kagan lumped children of these dispositions into a catchall "normal group" reflecting their being behaviorally easier to manage. Other researchers, notably Kiersey, corrected this error, though he often likes to speak of four pairs of temperaments, rather than just the classical four.

Introverted		Extroverted	
Melancholic	**Phlegmatic**	**Sanguine**	**Choleric**
More	→ less intense	←	More

Waldorf Education and the Four Temperaments

The understanding of the four temperaments used in Waldorf education is a sophisticated and developed one. Earlier in this century, Steiner reexamined the traditional view of the temperaments and was impressed by the wisdom it contained regarding human nature. He then refined these concepts and developed practical techniques based on the temperaments. Adults can use these to help understand and work on these behavior patterns (more will be said about this in the next chapter) and also to help children from being trapped in behavioral "dead ends" or bad habits. Adults can moderate the intensity of children's temperaments by helping them to break out of habitual tendencies.

The Melancholic Child
Thoughtful, sensitive, precise, drooping, moody, lonely

Dylan is a tall slim boy tending to paleness and having a transparent quality to his delicate skin. Despite his slight build, there can be a heaviness about him—he drags his feet and often slumps, though he is still years away from adolescence. At other times, however, he has a wiry fierceness and tenacity about him—he does not let go once he sets his mind to something. He is a moody and sensitive boy, disposed to moaning and whining, and can easily be moved to tears. This sensitivity, however, also manifests in empathy and concern for others. Sometimes this only shows in regards to animals, for he has a deep appreciation and love of nature. Dylan has excellent powers of observation, but can be obsessively self-observant to the point of paranoia, brooding, or hypochondria. This self-awareness can be extreme when he looks at his own body, especially as he gets older. He is overly cautious and has a tendency to fearfulness and phobias. This cautious attitude makes him a slow worker and a perfectionist in all that he does. He does not like the cold, and often he prefers the dark corner where he can pursue the hobbies in which he gets deeply involved, uninterested in the input of others. He has a delicate digestion and is easily prone to stomach aches, constipation and headaches.

Dylan plays the violin and does so not out of duty but out of real enjoyment. He has an acute sense of hearing, a gift for music, and excellent memory. Because the melancholic temperament has aptitude in the arts as well as a tremendous depth of feeling, many great musicians have been melancholics.

No person is a pure representative of one temperament. As we get older each of us manifest at least two—a primary one and a secondary one—the latter happily tending to balance the former, as one is normally introverted and the other, one of the extroverted temperaments. Certain combinations seem more common. The melancholic/choleric child tends to be egotistical, constantly irritated, socially difficult and high in energy—a handful for parents and teachers but oftentimes, a very successful person when grown up.

The melancholic child needs physical and emotional warmth. In dealing with her, the adult should be caring and sympathetic, patient but not caught up in her moods nor manipulated into satisfying her every whim. The melancholic child needs to be lifted from gloomy introspection by either focusing on others or by being given errands and household tasks where she can be helpful. Fairy tales, stories, and, as she gets older, biographies which portray others' struggles with life can stimulate the melancholic child to forget her own troubles. She can be at her best when attending to someone less fortunate. More than any other temperament, melancholics are interested in suffering and make the best nurses and caregivers.

The melancholic child is fond of sweets and even needs them more than other children when especially irritated. Steiner particularly recommended that they have oats (be it in porridge or granola) because the high oil content helped to warm them and to give them more energy.

The melancholic, like his fellow introvert the phlegmatic, can prefer staying indoors too much. Bringing the melancholic into an early connection with outdoor nature activities can inculcate a habit that overcomes this tendency. Thus encouraging him to be outside and to be engaged in physical activity is important.

The child also may need help in finding opportunities with other children. He is not naturally skilled in the social realm and has to have one-on-one playdates arranged so that these skills can be developed (teams and group activities develop a different set of skills). Otherwise he may get stuck in the solitude and loneliness he most prefers.

The Sanguine Child
Airy, light-filled, smiling, sociable, superficial, inconsistent, flighty

Erica is the archetype of the joyful, fun-filled child. She is lively, even vivacious, full of excitement and wonder. She meets each new experience with enthusiasm, though she never stays with any one thing for long. Childhood as a stage of life has an inherent sanguine quality, just as middle age has a phlegmatic cast and old age the depth as well as the heaviness of melancholia.

Erica is tall, blonde, and slim but better proportioned than the lanky melancholic child. She is light on her feet—her eurythmy teacher knew her temperament at once from the way in which she walks almost on her toes. She never wears out the heels on her shoes.

Erica can be witty and lighthearted, even bubbly, and is very popular, though her demands for constant change and diversion can become irritating. Boredom is what she fears most. With her effervescence, she always brings a smile to others. She sometimes disappoints her friends, though, because she is not dependable and lacks the follow-through to get things done. She forgets her promises and commitments to others or just fails to understand why that sort of thing is even important! Erica is a child of the whirlwind. Restless and usually in motion, she loves to dance and whirl about, to swing and to climb about on rocks and trees.

In the formal environment of school, this airiness can be a problem. Erica has difficulty with concentration and memory. Her thinking is neither systematic nor focused. Her mother complains that Erica usually manages to misplace or forget her homework assignments somewhere between school and home. She has difficulty sitting all day at her desk and is liable to break into a fit of giggling or to get into mischief just for diversion.

Parents and teachers must remember that one should never directly confront a child's temperament. A rigid attitude will not work with this child. Rather the adult needs to appreciate the world of the sanguine child and to enter it oneself in order to move the child along. Rather one tries to work with and guide or coax the child toward a more balanced direction. Hence, a parent should not simply try to force the sometimes scatterbrained sanguine child to do homework. Instead, arousing enthusiasm for the subject or the task is better, usually through participation of the parent. This will help the child learn to remain focused for longer periods of time. Television and other "screen time" are the worst thing for the sanguine child. Though they satisfy this child's desire for constant change and diversion, they only exacerbate the child's superficiality and ability to remain engaged.

Nutritionally, one might attempt to weigh the sanguine child down a bit. Whole grains are mandatory, especially wheat and rye. Good luck though in keeping this child from just nibbling at such hearty fare. For the sanguine child is quintessentially one without a care and without responsibility, living and loving life spontaneously and without regrets, taking each moment as it comes and quickly letting it go, leaving the slow and measured contemplation of life's depths and mysteries to others.

The Phlegmatic Child
Patient, even-tempered, harmonious, procrastinating, comfort-loving, lazy

Laura is an unashamedly chubby little girl. She loves food and she loves to eat. She is often dreaming of ice cream sundaes dripping with chocolate and marshmallow sauce and covered with whipped cream. In school her reverie might feature the lunch her mother packed and the possibility that, well, she might just tuck into it at snack time instead of waiting until noon.

There is a pervasive expansiveness and wateriness about Laura. She moves slowly but with a stolid grace, reminding one of a stately ship sailing in a steady breeze. Her thinking likewise is deliberate and methodical. She gets along with others because her nature is easygoing and she dislikes "making waves." She can be almost bovine in her placidity and imperturbability. Laura is able, though, to think deeply about things because she "chews" on them a bit before formulating an opinion. When Laura works, she is slow and steady and, like the tortoise who overcame the sanguine hare, she has perseverance and endurance. She can plod through a tedious and difficult task on which other children would soon give up on.

Though Laura is liked by her classmates, she has some social difficulties. She is sometimes teased about her weight—at her school there are few heavier children and she does stand out, especially in games class. But generally, she does not seem interested in doing many things. She needs the enthusiasm of her friends to get her fired up and she never gets around to initiating social activity on her own. Like the melancholic child, she needs parental help in organizing play dates and getting her involved with others. (But once she is involved, she loves it!)

One danger of the phlegmatic nature is the tendency to wallow in comfort and passivity, i.e., to become a couch potato. Also, phlegmatics have a hard time dealing with change. She can run into trouble, though, when quickness and alertness are called for. And never expect a quick answer from a reflective child like Laura. Even though she is bright, she is rarely spontaneous. The phlegmatic child can be depended on for faithfully practicing something and for memorization.

The phlegmatic child often needs to be spurred into action. Helping him to find a goal he sees as worthy of striving toward is one way of doing this. Waldorf teachers have a few other techniques that they use. One is to have all the phlegmatic children in the class to sit together. The other is to assign a phlegmatic child an exceedingly phlegmatic role in the class play. Both strategies overdose the child with his own temperament, thus coaxing him into behaviors and attitudes that are not typical for him and that help create balance. These two techniques work for other temperaments as well.

Steiner called phlegmatic children "sleeping cholerics." When suitably inspired they can explode into action, just as they can explode into anger when teased or tormented. Once being aroused, though, the phlegmatic soon settles back into her even-tempered manner.

The Choleric Child
Dynamic, energetic, action-oriented, pushy, insensitive, impetuous

Jeremy is a bundle of irrepressible energy who gets into one kind of mischief after another. He is stocky and square-shouldered, with dark, curly hair and a thick neck. He has a hyperactive quality about him but fortunately is too bright to be considered for the all-too-common Ritalin treatment. Jeremy has a quick temper but also a warm heart and a sociability that causes other children to admire and look up to him.

He likes to sleep late in the morning, but once he is up, he immediately wants action. He works and plays with passion and with force but he often lacks precision and form. Red is his favorite color, and his style is likewise brash, forthright, and unsubtle. This young Napoleon is a daredevil because he does not reflect enough to know fear—or even common sense at times. He is a child who lives in doing. As he gets older, though, he will learn to channel some of this vitality and become an excellent worker.

Generally speaking, an adult gets along most easily with children of his own temperament, you could say, because they speak the same language. A choleric adult knows the language of the choleric child and generally they get on well, but for other adults this child can be a trial. It is an effort to mobilize the fiery energy needed to meet the child on her own terms and then keep that energy under control. One can easily react with anger, which may not be the most helpful response.

The choleric child greatly appreciates the adult who has mastered a particular skill or technique and is willing to share that with the child. The child will work hard for such an adult and in the process learn to moderate tantrums and outbursts.

A very gifted eurythmy teacher appraised Jeremy the first day he walked—or rather stomped—into class. (The footprint a choleric child leaves in the sand is all heel!) She immediately made him her special child, a class pet. She gave him many kinds of helping tasks and challenged him with difficult rod exercises and moving quickly from one thing to the next. Jeremy's other teachers were astounded at how well behaved and motivated he was in eurythmy class. Their own response was to groan with foreboding when he was launched through the door of their classes and they braced themselves for his inevitable antics, even though these often left them chuckling. The other children in class were also amazed, never having thought of Jeremy as a teacher's favorite, especially in eurythmy.

Harnessing all that energy is a challenge with a choleric child, and it often involves lots of outdoor activity along with projects and adventures. Positive behavior management techniques may be used judiciously. Too many negative consequences, though, are not good for any child and can only work occasionally to repress the restlessness of the choleric. What he really needs is an adult who accepts and loves him for what he is and who, through effort and imagination, helps him channel his creative, if boisterous, energies.

Parents and teachers need the flexibility to enter into the particular temperament of a child and be that temperament for that child. They must learn to appeal to and relate to each of the temperaments. A bit of standard Waldorf wisdom is that when a teacher makes up and tells a story, she will win the attention of the choleric child by entering vigorously into the narration of the hero's battle with the seven-headed dragon. But she must include a magnificent banquet scene sensuously described to interest the phlegmatic child and a tragic scene poignantly depicted to arouse the sympathies of the melancholic. To be really successful in reaching the various temperaments, though, is more than a matter of technique. Rather, it involves a certain degree of self-knowledge and self-recognition—in terms of temperament, who am I as an adult? How one-sided is my approach to life, and how open am I to another perspective? The topic of how an adult's temperament affects a child is what we will explore next.

Watching Your Temper(ament)

On the very first day of the first training course that he gave for Waldorf teachers in 1919 (published as *Discussions with Teachers*), Rudolf Steiner stressed the need to honor the diversity of children's needs. Steiner was not so bothered about class size as long as the individuality of each child was addressed. In this regard, he indicated that "the most important task of the educator is to know and recognize these four types we call temperaments."

In Waldorf circles this "temperament work" has two aspects. The most obvious involves identifying the temperament of a child and then making interventions or adaptations of one's teaching or discipline style to match that temperament's style. This allows one to engage the interest of a child in a story or even a math lesson by playing to his or her temperament. On another level, some children can be overly "stuck" in just one style of learning or behavior and the right intervention can help them to broaden their repertoire. Some examples of this include choosing an overly choleric child and seating her with all the other cholerics until all this "choler" becomes a bit too much for them all, or by choosing a very phlegmatic role for an already very phlegmatic child in the class play. Both of these "homeopathic" ("like repels like") interventions can work to shake the child out of his characteristic constitution and open him to trying something else. A skilled teacher has something in each lesson that appeals to each temperament and is also able to draw out and develop the special gift of each temperament. Thus the children learn to appreciate the strengths and virtues of those who are different from them.

The other approach to temperament work is equally important but perhaps more difficult. It requires that the teacher or parent take note of and then work on his *own* temperamental style. Balancing the excesses of this very intimate (and too often ignored) part of who we are constitutes an important path in our self development and has an important bearing not only in our interactions with our children but also in those with our friends, colleagues, and spouses.

Modern psychologists speak of the "goodness of fit" between the child's temperament and the values of the adult in the child's life. The psychiatrist and bestselling author on parenting, Stanley Turecki, tells the story of a young, very active girl who could be aggressive, a choleric child. Living on a rural Midwest farm in a home with relatively few demands besides helping with the farm work, her rough and tumble style netted her the reputation of being "a tomboy." This same child, however, if transported to a small Manhattan apartment lovingly filled with prize antiques, the home of two busy professionals with high demands on their child's academic performance and behavior, would find a very different outcome. Here the child would no doubt be diagnosed with ADHD and medicated.

As parents and teachers, we need to realize that our particular temperament can affect "goodness of fit" for ourselves and our children. By recognizing and understanding our own temperament, we can create a home and school environment that will serve the growing child.

The Melancholic Adult

The melancholic adult is very aware of her physical body. The melancholic (referred to by some psychologists as the "highly sensitive person," since the term "melancholic" has a negative connotation for some) has a low threshold for discomfort and pain and often is plagued by ailments that others can just shrug off. Allergies, headaches, abdominal problems and digestive difficulties are common afflictions. and either because of all this or in response, she can be overly thin and insufficiently robust. She is frequently at the doctor and is likely to be an enthusiast for every new health diet and alternative therapy. Some doctors frame these difficulties in term of neurotransmitter imbalances and suggest a treatment like Prozac. In general, though temperament does not respond to such treatment.

When it comes to interactions with children, the melancholic excels at offering lots of care and attention as well as an avid interest in all that may ail the child—they are always interested in ailments. The danger is that this caring can be overdone and become controlling or overprotective. The melancholic may project her own frailty and sensitivity onto her child, not allowing him enough outdoor play and keeping him from adventures that involve risk. This can suppress a child's natural need to explore and experiment. It can cause the child to retreat and not fully express himself. Melancholics are also perfectionists, holding themselves and their children to very high standards. This can also make for a stifling regime, especially if applied too early in a child's development.

Interestingly, even children of typically extroverted temperament—the sanguines and cholerics—tend to become more introverted when raised by melancholic parents. Melancholic parents need to compensate for this "social blind spot" by taking initiative in arranging frequent playdates and one-on-one social situations for their children. They need to be careful about projecting their own introversion and social reticence onto their children. Children need to develop essential social skills. This aspect of "emotional intelligence" is very important for later happiness and success.

The melancholic adult, having a well developed inner life of feeling, usually wants to have a deep, personal relationship with her child. To her bewilderment and dismay, the child—particularly the extroverted youngster—may have no interest in such a relationship and may even be irritated by the attention and push the parent away. The melancholic parent needs to find a balance between hovering over the child and letting the child be.

A final danger is that chronic depression, which often afflicts the unbalanced melancholic temperament, can be passed from parent to child. There is about a forty percent correlation between depression in mothers and later problems with depression for their children. Thus melancholic adults need to consciously develop elements of other temperamental styles in their own thoughts and behavior. Melancholic parents are potentially the best parents. They are caring, attentive and interested in their children. They try to meet what they perceive their child's needs to be and are good disciplinarians. They just need to lighten up a bit, focus on the joys of parenting, and remember the importance of social interaction.

The Choleric Adult

The choleric person, possessing " the temperament of fire" is referred to by some psychologists as the "active" temperament. Though warm-heartedness is also a trait he possesses, the choleric is generally better known for being impulsive, workaholic, and prickly. Action is what he lives for, and other people can sometimes be viewed merely as tools for accomplishing what the choleric wants done. He tends to be the least sensitive of the temperaments especially in terms of reading the needs of others. This is mainly because he is so focused, with almost tunnel vision, on achieving a goal. Cholerics are people who get things done.

In relating to children, the choleric adult is action-orientated. He likes to plan projects and lead adventures and can be lots of fun. He is high in energy and can accomplish a tremendous amount, be it in the classroom, the playing field or the home. But he is usually more interested in his own ideas and aims than in those of others. He lacks the sensitivity and ability to listen and to tune into the needs of children. The choleric also tends to be more interested in what a child does and can do than in what a child needs or feels.

It is hard for the choleric to be rhythmical and steady, and this often shows the most when it comes to managing discipline—he tends to be to harsh one moment and uninterested or unavailable the next. The choleric adult has a tendency to be domineering and overwhelming which, for a sensitive or inward child, can evoke submission and even fear. Such a regimen can traumatize a young child leading to nervousness, no doubt from living in constant anticipation of again being "blasted" by the choleric caregiver's outbursts (even if they are directed to someone other than the child). On the physical level, such children can also develop breathing problems. However, even their organ formation can be compromised, and later in life, these children can have problems with poor digestion and metabolic disorders as well.

The choleric style of child-rearing, like the other temperament styles, is not necessarily limited to those adults of that particular temperament. Until the late 1960s, the choleric approach was more or less standard in North America. Parents of non-choleric persuasion adopted this strong, insensitive, quasi-military approach that deemed that children are to be dominated and are meant "to be seen and not heard." Since then as a society we have come to react to such excesses and have now taken on a more phlegmatic or sanguine approach to children's upbringing But as we shall see, these two less intense styles also have their dangers.

The Sanguine Adult

The sanguine person is by nature light, carefree, fun-loving and optimistic. Although the cholerics get a lot more done and the melancholics do a more careful and complete job, the sanguine is often the most popular and successful person. The sanguine does not get bogged down in one thing, avoids the overly abstract or the overly serious, and moves from one experience or friendship to the next, rather like the beautiful butterfly tasting the nectar of many lovely flowers.

All children have a bit of the playful, fun-loving nature of the sanguine, and the sanguine adult can bring much joy and entertainment to children. There are potential problems though. The child has other deeper needs and especially non-sanguine children can have difficulty keeping up with the overly sanguine adult. Too much of this flitting about with constant shopping and excursions and activities can create a psychological exhaustion. The child never learns to be aroused inwardly—he is seduced into a life that is overly shallow and too much focused on constantly changing outer impressions. This becomes a child with attention problems or a boy who is easily seduced by computer games and videos or a girl obsessed with fashion and shopping. Such children rarely get in touch with their deeper side, do not develop a strong will, and may lack a vitality and zest for life that stems from within. For such children adolescence can be very trying because they are unable to find content in their lives at this crucial developmental stage which is so concerned with finding meaning.

Because sanguine adults often start many things but find it hard to bring anything to completion, they can be messy housekeepers (though with the quantity of "stuff" that every home now finds essential, most of us are beginning to tend in this direction). Recent studies have indicated that a home can be a bit unclean but that if things are constantly scattered about and rarely picked up and put in order, a child's thinking develops in this similarly scattered and disorganized manner, marring later academic achievement. Some people attribute the Waldorf preschool's attention to orderliness at the end of each day to some notion of propriety but the fruits of this practice support both healthy neurological development and a sense of stability and order.

The sanguine adult has difficulty heeding the child's need for a regular, predictable, harmonious life. Having regular mealtimes and bedtimes is obviously important, but for the sanguine may in practice be difficult to realize. Providing consistent limits and discipline is also not a high priority for the sanguine, often focused on enjoying himself. Consciously incorporating a degree of the melancholic's sensitivity to the child's needs, attention to detail, and follow-through can bring real balance.

The Phlegmatic Adult

The easy-going phlegmatic values comfort and non-confrontation but can slip into laziness and indifference. The phlegmatic is loyal, consistent (sometimes to the point of monotony), anchored and dependable. The watery phlegmatic way with its even and rhythmical habits is a balm and a support, especially to the preschool child. This temperament brings many good qualities to parenting and to teaching but also has its dangers.

The typical child is bursting with vitality and looks to the adult for help and for model behaviors in finding ways to channel energy. An overly-phlegmatic adult can dampen this energy and leave the child's soul "asphyxiated." Where the child wants to be active, to explore or to create, it is met by dullness, by tiredness, by ennui which over time promotes a child who is dull and not interested in anything. That "couch potato" parent harms more than his own waistline by his inactivity.

Too phlegmatic an approach can also leave a child insufficiently cared for or attended. The phlegmatic adult can focus too much on his or her own comfort or what is easiest for him or her and not be attuned to the less obvious needs of children. Their "don't sweat the small stuff" attitude may make them poor disciplinarians or guides for their children. To maximize their potential, many children need a certain degree of "push" from the adults around them—getting them to practice the violin, do homework, try new things, even to do their best. They need constant monitoring, encouragement, and help. While some temperaments can overdo this, the phlegmatic is at risk for doing too little. Plodding along in the same old way can, on one hand, provide a comforting security blanket for the child (this is the forte of the mellow plegmatic), but such a style needs to be modified if one is to provide the child's will the challenges it needs to meet the future.

No temperament is good or bad. Each is a mixture of possible strengths and weaknesses. We all need to develop the positive sides of our particular temperaments and consciously cultivate the positive qualities of the other temperaments. The first step is to identify what temperament we are. As adults we normally have a primary and then a secondary temperament. To identify your primary temperament, first look at the physique which typifies most of your adult life: lean and wiry = melancholic, thick-necked and stocky = choleric, rounded = phlegmatic, and slim and balanced = sanguine. If the primary temperament is one of the extroverted types (sanguine or choleric), the secondary temperament is almost always one of the introverted ones (and vice versa).

Once you become aware of your types, get acquainted with the typical strengths and weaknesses that go along with those styles. In this exploration of temperament, you will have increasing "aha!" experiences as you recognize that temperament is the reason you mother or your spouse or your daughter does things or sees things in a particular way. Farther down the line one can start to work on the reason for this exercise, which is to understand the way temperament influences your own habits.

Having gotten this far you now have the possibility of making a choice—should I go along with my usual temperament's way of doing things or should I expand my habitual repertoire and do it a little differently? Every temperament has its gift and its biases. For the classroom, Steiner spoke of the need for the teacher to learn to become whatever temperament the child needs at that time. As parents (or even spouses or co-workers), we can lazily and unconsciously just go along with our usual way of interacting with others or we can attempt to practice being another temperament, thus stretching ourselves and developing a more alive and flexible being.

Temperament has a physiological basis connected to our physical gestalt and neurotransmitter levels. It is not an immutable determinant of behavior. Over time we can with conscious effort adopt any temperament in a situation and become a harmonious blending of the four.

A Modern Path of Meditation and Inner Development

According to Rudolf Steiner, there are two dimensions of reality. One is the physical, material world that the human being perceives with the physical senses of sight, hearing, touch, and so forth. The other is the invisible and impalpable spiritual realm that lies behind the physical world. This is comprised of the subtle energies, elemental nature beings, and higher spiritual beings that have brought the physical world into being and that animate, influence, and direct it. In past ages, human beings were able to perceive and communicate, in varying degrees, with this spiritual world. For the modern human being, particularly for the Western person, this domain is a closed *terra incognita*. The materialistic worldview that prevails in much of our culture holds that this domain does not exist, that all invisible realities are merely epiphenomena of matter. Agnostics hold that while this world may exist, the human being has no capacity to perceive or enter into it.

On the first page of his book *Knowledge of the Higher Worlds: A Modern Path of Initiation*, Steiner writes that within each human being lies dormant the capacity to perceive, experience and communicate with the spiritual realm. He then describes a series of exercises in meditation and inner work that, if practiced regularly and with enthusiasm, will bring the seeker experience of this world.

The meditative path that Steiner describes and that he also calls "spiritual research" has a strong moral element. He asserts that for each step forward that a person takes in meditative practice, one must take three steps in moral development. Also, a person's impulse to follow this path must arise, not out of selfish motives, but out of a wish to benefit all of humanity. The ultimate aim of this way of meditation is not to escape from the world and the cycle of birth, suffering, and death but to be able to live in the world with new powers of insight and creativity and to help improve the world. Human destiny is inextricably tied to the destiny of the earth.

Steiner acknowledges the richness and effectiveness of the meditative traditions of the East (of India, China, Tibet, Japan and others) but holds that they may not be the most appropriate for the modern person, especially the Westerner. Many of these Asian techniques are based on the control of the breath and may require renunciation of the world. The meditative practice Steiner presents is based on the control and discipline of the thinking process and is meant to be pursued in the midst of life.

The spiritual practice that Steiner describes involves a training and development of both the heart and the mind. One prerequisite for spiritual work is an attitude of veneration, a devotion to truth and knowledge, not for one's own sake, but for the sake of others. This mood of devotional reverence requires that we be open-minded, patient, and positive, and that we refrain from criticism of others. These attributes help create an inward receptiveness without which even the most dedicated mental exertions would not bear fruit. Regular meditation itself helps one develop these attributes, but often they in themselves require some concentrated work and attention. Prayer, religious practice, artistic therapies, and psychotherapy can help here.

The discipline of the mind begins with the study of spiritual texts. This helps to moderate our normal, materialistic and narrow way of looking at the world. Such study also helps to develop our powers of both mental and feeling concentration.

The next step is to make thinking more conscious and to gain control over the thinking process. This is necessary if one is to gain access to the spiritual domain. In meditation the aim is to shed our body-based consciousness and to cross the "threshold" that separates our everyday consciousness from the realm of imagination and spirit. The threshold is a semi-permeable boundary that protects our normal consciousness from intrusions of the subconscious and the superconscious, from both demons and angels, so we can go about our daily lives. Without such a boundary our consciousness would like the "magical realism" of Latin American novels and films or even one of mental illness.

According to Steiner, when we sleep, or more accurately, when the body sleeps, the nonphysical aspects of our being—the soul and spirit—enter the spiritual world. Normally we do not remember much of what transpires on these nightly sojourns, but some of our dreams can be understood as memories of what happened there. During these times out thinking is not clear or focused because we what we experience impacts more the nonverbal realm of feeling. Occasionally these dreams lend inspiration to the artist. It does not generally help us so much in dealing with our personal problems and those we are dealing with in the world. For such a purpose, we need to gain access to the inspiration of the higher worlds in a more awake fashion.

There are means other than sleep by which we cross the threshold. Psychedelic drugs, a high fever, chanting, breathing exercises, ecstatic dance, and so on can induce an experience of the unseen world but usually one that is dreamy, unfocused and characterized by fleeting images, colors, or flights of fantasy. Typically, in such experiences the emotions are highly aroused, and one's thinking is neither clear nor objective. These experiences can be pleasurable (most experiences that feel good involve some degree of "leaving our body"), but they do not tend to be useful—it is our thinking and cognition that need to be inspired for this to be so. We need to be able to cross the threshold while continuing to be able to think in a clear and focused way.

The first task for the meditator is, in Steiner's words, to "build a hut" on the other side of the threshold. In this protected space one can be open to receive spiritual impressions but still have one's consciousness "held in" and condensed rather than dissipated. This is what usually occurs when one enters the realm of dreams, imagination, and invisible beings. This hut is constructed through strengthening one's thinking so that when one crosses over, one can both maintain a wakened consciousness and remember what one experiences there. The control of thinking is strengthened through concentration exercises.

One of the basic concentration exercises Steiner recommends consists of choosing a simple, human-made object—a pencil, a pin, a match, a paper clip—and focusing one's thinking on it. One may think only thoughts related to the object. All extraneous thoughts need to be excluded but for the mental picture of the paper clip. One maintains this focus through such inner questions as: What is it made of? How was it made? What was the intent of its inventor? Where was it manufactured? And so on. Thus one always keeps the mind on the topic of the paper clip. Unrelated thoughts and feelings will break in, but one must persistently return to the theme. One strives to develop a well-structured sequence of thoughts in order to foster absolutely clear thinking.

This concentration exercise does not sound very challenging, but it is. Steiner recommends that it should be practiced every day for five to ten minutes, but most beginners find it difficult to hold a single line of though for that long. The ability to complete the exercise comes with daily practice and many find the "paper clip exercise" a useful tool when they need grounding, as before beginning a meeting or going to a job interview. It also makes an excellent warm-up before a session of regular meditation. It is an essential exercise, because if one wants to learn to bring clear thoughts out of the realm of inspired imagination, one must first be capable of thinking clear thoughts.

When one has developed some ability to concentrate, one can start to learn to meditate. Meditation in the Western tradition is quite different from the Eastern traditions which have become popular in recent years: mindfulness practices, transcendental meditation, and so on. In the Western tradition one often works with words and sentences that one thinks about and understands. Hence, the practice of contemplative reflection begins with verses or short sentences of an inspirational nature. One practice verse that Steiner suggested for beginners is: *Wisdom lives in the light.* One can, however, choose verses, and later, paragraphs and longer passages-from the Bible, from other scriptures of the East and West, from the writings of religious thinkers and mystics as well as from the literature of Anthroposophy. In this, one goes beyond normal, everyday thinking through steeping oneself in the lofty thoughts conceived in moments of meditation by spiritual seekers who have been inspired by the spirit.

In this so-called "word meditation," one begins by taking a theme and merely trying to understand what it means. If we do not understand something, then we can meditate in this style to reach an understanding. One must actively ponder the thought, not just say the words over and over. One might then condense the thought and focus on a key word. In Steiner's practice verse, for example, one can hold the image of *the light* and at the same time fold the concepts of *wisdom* and *lives in* into it. Also, one might compare various meanings of light, both physical and metaphorical, as well as visualize things associated with light.

Eventually, this concentrated thinking or contemplating of the theme leads to another stage. At a certain moment the theme begins "to think itself," to generate new pictures and images that are not the products of associative memory or of "old thinking." At this moment one has begun true meditation.

In word meditation, there are two principal challenges. One is to get beyond the thought, to make the leap to imaginatively playing with the thought or seeing it pictorially—to think it without words. The practical-minded person who thinks in concrete terms and the very intense person (like many cholerics) both have trouble doing this. Their challenge is to be flexible enough to move into the phase of being open and receptive. Steiner felt that the scientifically-trained person has great potential for meditation because the mind has already been trained to think clearly. However, in meditation one also needs the ability to surrender control and be open to what comes toward one. Steiner called this quality "the reversed will" where one paradoxically must bring intense effort into the act of ceding control. Artistic work, especially movement and the composing of poetry, can help to overcome this rigidity or resistance to surrender. Steiner also gave a set of "perceptual meditation" practices that can help in this regard.

The opposite challenge is faced by the person who strays beyond the bounds of the protective hut and, rather than seeking clear and defined mental pictures and thoughts, revels in and gets lost in feelings or in vague sensations of the soul. The exercise becomes a kind of daydreaming on the theme. Usually, more consequent practice of the concentration exercise can correct this. Also, there are other meditation exercises that Steiner prescribed for learning to control excessive feeling, his so-called "subsidiary exercises." Diet, exercise, and specific therapeutic interventions can also help an individual become more grounded.

Meditation can be done with others, and it is often helpful to be part of a group that meets regularly. Group meditation can give new energy and focus to the work of each person. Many people find it easier to meditate while in a group. In groups, individuals can share their experiences in meditation, receive advice and encouragement from others, and gain confidence in the value of their inner experiences. For those unable to find a working group, Steiner recommended keeping a meditation journal in which one records one's experiences in order to give them clarity and objective form.

As one progresses in this meditative practice, and the hut becomes well-established in the realm of imagination and spirit, one can focus on specific questions or problems. Using the model of "word meditation," one can meditate upon and await an inspiration related to a question regarding one's professional or personal life. Especially important are questions related to one's lifework, to the problems for which we are seeking solution on the behalf of others. Steiner called this "spiritual research." He held that the challenges that modern humanity faces can be met only when we use this method to gain help and inspiration from the spiritual world.

Steiner made it very clear that this path of meditation and inner development is a fundamental spiritual activity and not tied to any particular religious tradition. One can be a Buddhist, Christian, Muslim, Jew, Hindu, or any other faith and pursue this path without compromising one's other spiritual and religious activities. Steiner also held that persons in any field of endeavor could and should meditate. A gardener, scientist, lawyer, laborer, and craftperson all, through meditation, can develop concentration and clarity of mind, as well as receive new thoughts and inspirations that will help them with their work.

As the founder of Waldorf education, Steiner held that meditation is a necessary element in the life of the teacher and in the life of the school. Only through meditation can the teacher come to "living thoughts" that will allow him or her to present the Waldorf curriculum in a vital and engaging way and to deal with the demands and challenges of being a teacher. For Steiner, the path of inner development is a *sine qua non* of being a Waldorf teacher.

Steiner suggested certain meditations for teachers. He recommended that each night before going to sleep a teacher visualize each child in the class. In effect, the teacher, in doing this, poses a question to the invisible world: What can I do to best meet the needs of this child? Novice teachers should understand, though, that Steiner gave this exercise to a group of advance meditators (whose "huts" were well established). They were already trained to sense-free thinking. To make this exercise meaningful and effective, one must be seriously working on a broader meditative practice.

In a number of Waldorf schools, the weekly teachers' meetings begin with either a concentration exercise or a short meditation. This can help each person to listen more fully to the others and to be more occupied with the well-being of the group and of the school, rather than with his or her own personal agenda.

Many systems of meditation focus on achieving the highest level of enlightenment, the overcoming of subject and object, the sense of unity with all that exists, and with infinity and eternity. Rudolf Steiner's approach to meditation is unique in that it focuses on attaining practical insights from lower stories of the ascending tower of higher consciousness. Simple and direct, and requiring an amount of time and effort that even busy persons of today can manage, this discipline can help almost anyone to enliven and spiritualize daily life and work. It can also in time lead to the higher levels of consciousness. Consistent practice is slowly and subtly life-transforming, leading not only to knowledge and vision, but to a life that is more humane and more meaningful.

Steiner was once traveling by rail in Central Europe, and the train stopped at a small, rural village. Steiner turned to his traveling companions and commented, "There is a man who has been meditating by himself in this village for many years. The entire area has been subtly changed because of this." Our meditative practice can be a blessing to ourselves and also to those around us.